Sunset

LANDSCAPING SMALL SPACES

BY HAZEL WHITE AND THE EDITORS OF SUNSET BOOKS

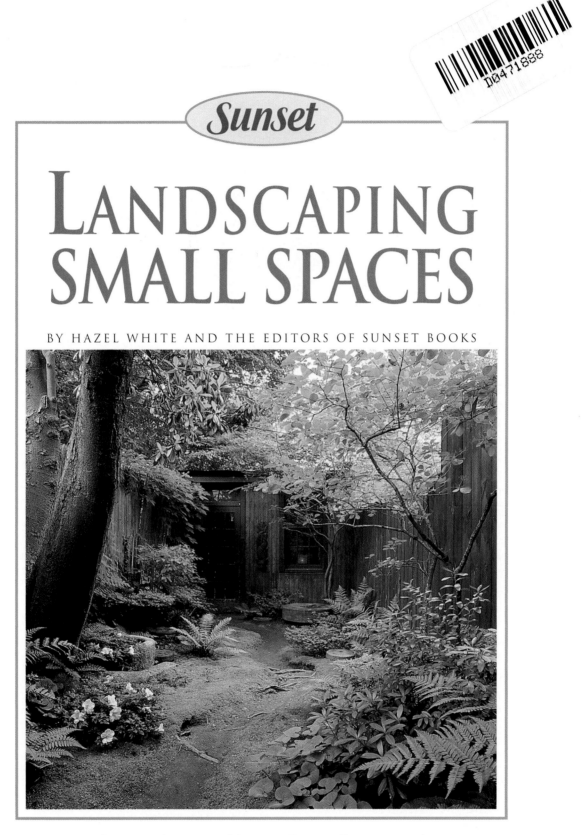

SUNSET BOOKS · MENLO PARK, CALIFORNIA

POCKETS OF PARADISE

The size of an average garden is shrinking. The private gardens in many new suburban developments are no larger than urban gardens. Instead of gracious open spaces around our homes, most of us have pocket-size pieces of earth—or perhaps just an entryway or a roof—that may at first seem unlikely places for making a private paradise.

Yet, as this book shows, you can build a beautiful garden—even one that feels close to nature and far from the pressures of life—in a small space. Some of the gardens pictured here are as tiny as a balcony with a single chair facing the sun; some have space for a permanent outdoor table for entertaining in the fresh air; others have the

luxury of several small, distinct garden areas, allowing for places to explore and different outdoor activities.

It's vital in these times of dwindling green space that gardeners continue to create comfortable outdoor spaces where people can relax and feel connected to the natural world. The chapters in this book will encourage you to do that and demonstrate how you can achieve more than you ever imagined—even if your garden were two or three times as large.

We would like to thank John R. Dunmire for reviewing the chapter on shopping for plants and Scott Atkinson for his advice on building arbors and other garden structures.

SUNSET BOOKS

Vice President, General Manager: Richard A. Smeby
Vice President, Editorial Director: Bob Doyle
Production Director: Lory Day
Art Director: Vasken Guiragossian

Staff for this book:

Managing Editor: Joan Beth Erickson
Sunset Books Senior Editor, Gardening: Marianne Lipanovich
Copy Editor: Julie Harris
Indexer: Barbara J. Braasch
Photo Researcher: Kathleen Olson
Production Coordinator: Patricia S. Williams
Assistant Editor: Bridget Biscotti Bradley

Art Director: Alice Rogers
Illustrator: Rik Olson
Computer Production: Linda Bouchard

Cover: Photography by Saxon Holt. Garden design by Suzanne Porter.
Border photograph by Claire Curran.

For additional copies of *Landscaping Small Spaces* or any other Sunset book, call 1-800-526-5111 or visit our web site at *www.sunsetbooks.com*

PHOTOGRAPHERS:

Marion Brenner: 79, 106 middle, bottom, 107 middle; **Karen Bussolini:** 11 bottom right, 19 bottom right, 21 bottom right, 46 top; **David Cavagnaro:** 13 bottom right, 43 top right, 47 middle left, 94 top, 110 top; **Glenn Christiansen:** 89; **Eric Crichton/ The Garden Picture Library:** 20 top left; **Claire Curran:** 39 bottom right, 42 bottom, 100 top, 104 bottom, 107 bottom; **Janet Davis:** 98 bottom; **Arnaud Descat/ M.A.P.:** 20 bottom right, 47 bottom left, 52 top; **Alan & Linda Detrick:** 38 bottom, 51 bottom right; **F. Didillon/M.A.P.:** 25 bottom right, 43 middle left, 45 top right; **Derek Fell:** 25 bottom middle, 49 middle left, 57 middle right, bottom left, 67, 91, 97 bottom; **Roger Foley:** 1, 3 bottom left, 11 bottom left, 15 bottom right, 16 top left, 17 bottom right, 19 top right, 21 top right, 25 top right, 28 top, 29 top left, 34 top left, middle left, 35 bottom left, 37 bottom right, 44 top, 45 bottom left, 46 bottom right, 47 top right, bottom right, 49 top right, 54 top, 55 top left, top right, bottom right, 56 top, middle, 92, 96 top; **Alain Guerrier/M.A.P.:** 41 bottom right; **Steven Gunther:** 13 top left, 17 top left, 30 bottom left, 31 top right, 48 top, 49 bottom; **Mick Hales/GreenWorld Pictures, Inc.:** 13 bottom left; **Harry Haralambou:** 43 bottom right; **Jerry Harpur:** 3 top right, 8, 12 top left, 15 top right, 19 top left, 21 top left, 23 top right, bottom left, 24 top left, top right, bottom, 29 middle left, bottom left, 33 bottom right, 35 top left, 38 top right, 43 bottom left, 45 bottom left, 51 top left, 53 top left; **Marcus Harpur:** 17 top right, 32 top; **Lynne Harrison:** 7 bottom, 25 bottom left, 29 bottom right, 30 top left, 41 top, 42 top right, 44 middle, 53 bottom right, 54 bottom, 57 top, 61, 85, back cover top left; **Sunniva Harte/The Garden Picture Library:** 50 bottom; **Marijke Heuff/The Garden Picture Library:** 25 top left; **Saxon Holt:** 3 middle right, bottom right, 18, 31 bottom right, 33 bottom left, 37 top right, 58, 102, 109 middle; **Andrew Lawson:** 34 middle right, 41 middle right, 48 bottom; **Allan Mandell:** 5, 28 bottom, 35 bottom right, 77, 99, back cover bottom left; **Charles Mann:** 12 top right, bottom, 13 top right, 15 bottom left, 16 bottom right, 30 top right, 31 top left, 38 top left, 44 bottom, 48 middle, 52 bottom, 53 top right, bottom left, 55 middle left, 87, 95, 100 bottom, 104 middle, 109 bottom; **Mayer/Le Scanff/The Garden Picture Library:** 40 bottom; **N. and P. Mioulane/ M.A.P.:** 21 bottom left, 42 top left, 52 middle, 57 bottom right; **Ncum/M.A.P.:** 22; **Noun/M.A.P.:** 14, 33 middle right, 56 bottom, 101 bottom; **Hugh Palmer:** 3 top left, 4, 11 top right, 16 top right, 20 top right, bottom left, 33 top right, 50 top right, 96 middle, 97 top, 98 top; **Jerry Pavia:** 6, 29 top right, 47 top left, 101 top, 105 middle; **Norman A. Plate:** 7 top; **Matthew Plut:** 3 middle left, 16 bottom left, 19 bottom left, 21 top middle, 26, 31 bottom left, 36 middle, 39 top left, 51 top right, bottom left, 55 bottom right, 65, 76, 81, 83, back cover right; **John Rizzo:** 69; **Susan A. Roth:** 11 top left, 33 top left, 34 bottom, 36 top, 37 top left, 39 top right, 45 top left, 49 top left, 73, 110 bottom; **Chad Slattery:** 96 bottom; **Friedrich Strauss/The Garden Picture Library:** 2, 15 top left, 23 top left; **Ron Sutherland/The Garden Picture Library:** 32 bottom, 63; **Michael S. Thompson:** 10, 17 bottom left, 30 bottom right, 36 bottom, 39 bottom left, 40 top, 43 top left, 46 bottom left, 105 bottom; **Juliette Wade/The Garden Picture Library:** 23 bottom right; **Peter O. Whiteley:** 71; **Tom Woodward:** 104 top, 105 top, 106 top, 107 top, 108 top, 109 top, 111 top; **Cynthia Woodyard:** 110 middle; **Steven Wooster/ The Garden Picture Library:** 35 top right, 43 middle right, 50 top left.

CONTENTS

INTRODUCTION TO
LANDSCAPING

The art of landscaping is usually learned from small beginnings. Without the opportunity to plant a grand avenue of trees along the driveway, you figure out instead how to choose and place one or two trees beautifully. You make a modest flower garden instead of a border 100 feet long, and learn the way the colors come and go and what satisfies the eye day after day.

The rewards of making a garden are more or less the same whether your garden is large or small. An amazing array of plants can grow there through the year, announcing the seasons and recording the weather by the way they bend in the breeze or collect raindrops on their buds and flowers. No matter what your garden's size, you and your guests can delight in exploring the different garden spaces and details, then sit down and relax, leaving the cares of the world a long way behind.

Small gardens have advantages over large ones. The atmosphere is usually by necessity intimate and secluded, and every detail of a pot or a flower can be appreciated up close. You can perhaps indulge a love of fine materials and objects and be glad you need only a few. Most important, a small yard offers the best chance of experimenting playfully or artistically with what you learn and what you like, while leaving you a little free time simply to sit outdoors in the fresh air.

SAVE YOUR PLANT IDEAS

Most gardens, unless they are professionally designed, get started with impulse nursery purchases. Vegetables are placed in a sunny spot for the season and shrubs are set out along the fence for now, until a better place comes to mind. Usually, without any plan ever being made for the garden as a whole, more and more spontaneously purchased plants gradually fill every inch of growing room.

During the planning of your garden, or while you are deliberating over a remodel, it's best to put the plant shopping on hold if you can. Fill a folder with plant photos from magazines and catalogs, visit gardens and take plant photographs, research all your favorites, but don't start planting before you have organized just what kinds of spaces go where.

THINK ABOUT SPACES

A successful garden has glorious spaces that people remember—perhaps a bench along a path out of the wind or a patio where dappled light plays over the tablecloth all through lunch. Even though you may be determined to maximize the planting opportunities in your garden, if you want the garden to be used and appreciated, commit yourself to allocating a generous amount of it to paths and sitting areas. To find out what makes these spaces comfortable, turn to the chapter "The Structure of a Small Garden."

FACING PAGE: A small path off the main one meanders between myriad different plants. ABOVE: A comfortable space for eating invites people to enjoy the garden.

DOODLE A PLAN

To landscape a garden well, plan first for these garden spaces—a sitting area and paths, as well as perhaps a lawn, a vegetable garden, a pond, fruit trees, and a children's play area. Give the sitting area priority. Depending on the size of your space and what you want, a sitting area might be a formal dining terrace or a hammock. Find your favorite places in the garden and delegate those as possible sites. For information on whether the perfect site is close to the house or away from it, see pages 14–17 and 60–61.

Now draw a plan on paper so that you can play with ways to connect the sitting area to other garden spaces and to the house. First make a base plan on graph paper. Measure the boundaries of the garden and the length of the house walls, then transfer the dimensions onto the paper, using a scale of ¼ or ½ inch for 1 foot. Mark the positions of the house windows and doors on the plan.

This garden includes a beautiful repetition of circles: round patio, round table with round pebbles on it, and plants trimmed into loose, round mounds.

Design: Sarah Hammond

Tape a sheet of tracing paper over the base plan and draw the sitting area on the tracing paper. Now the fun begins: trying to fit everything you want in your garden into the space you have. Try not to think about positioning certain plants yet. Instead concentrate on getting garden areas on the plan.

At first, including everything you want won't seem even remotely possible. There will be much demand for the sunny areas of the garden, which is probably where your sitting area is, and you'll be tempted to reduce the sitting area's size. But keep doodling on more overlays of tracing paper until you find a solution that keeps that space intact. The fruit trees can perhaps be espaliered on a fence, and the pond might become a series of large water pots around the garden that double as focal points (see pages 36–39). The two middle chapters of this book, "Creating a Sense of Spaciousness" and "Making the Most of Small Spaces," contain hundreds of ideas on how to expand your options. As you'll see, successful small gardens are full of ingenuity.

Don't forget to check the connections between the house and the garden. Will the garden views from the house doors and windows lure you outside? Are the house exits connected to the garden with comfortably wide paths or a small patio? A garden that seems separate from the house isn't used often.

The simplest garden plans are usually the most effective: a straight path through two or more garden spaces to a focal point, such as a tall urn or a water feature; or a circular path around the lawn with places to stop along the way. To establish a sense of unity, designers often repeat a shape throughout a garden: rectangular deck, rectangular pond; circular pond and semicircular seat; diagonal path, diagonal pattern on the fence, diamond-shaped pots. The shape may be taken from the lines of the house—bay windows, for example, might suggest a pattern of circles.

PLAN FOR PLANTS

In professionally designed small gardens, plantings may go on the plan last but they have been planned for. In every planning decision you make about your garden, consider the planting opportunities. For example, paths and patios with gaps between the stones can be planted; crevices in dry-stone walls can be planted; fences, arbor posts, tree trunks, and freestanding pillars can be draped with plants; containers can be placed atop walls,

In a small city garden, hundreds of lush plants of different heights grow in the ground and in pots and hang from the trees.

Design: David Feix

columns, and balustrades, on broad steps and in patio corners; and so on. Consider every surface, vertical as well as horizontal. And layer your plantings: shrubs under trees, small shrubs beneath tall ones, ground covers and bulbs below small shrubs. It's possible to shoehorn thousands of plants into a city garden. The plant lists in the chapter "Shopping for Plants" will help you get started.

REMODEL AS NEEDED

A little remodeling is required almost every year in a small garden. The trees, shrubs, and vines must be pruned to maintain the views out of the garden and to ensure a pleasing balance of sunlight and shade in the sitting areas; the paths must be kept clear; and the focal points should be bright and eye-catching. Sometimes this necessitates removing or replacing plants, and you mustn't hesitate to do that or the atmosphere of the garden will decline.

Old brick and mature vines are usually well worth saving during a remodel because they make the garden look as if it's always been there. An entirely new garden may take years to look settled in.

Design: Stephanie Feeney

A sure sign that the garden needs remodeling is if it is not being used. This may be due to poor connections between the house and garden (see "Doodle a Plan" on the facing page) or several other factors, such as awkward-shaped spaces, too much shade, or poor soil that prevents plants from thriving. Turn to the chapter "Designing around Obstacles" for help on a range of challenges often found in small gardens.

At the beginning of a remodel, don't move too quickly to tear out existing garden features. Everything that can't be made to work must go, but spend time trying to save anything that gives the garden a sense of age or individuality; for example, mature trees and shrubs, materials with an aged patina (including old concrete), a natural swale or slope, even an inherited collection of kitschy pots. The history of the garden can be of interest; only as a last resort build a brand new world there.

THE STRUCTURE OF A
SMALL GARDEN

Small or large, a garden needs good structure. The look of the garden may be soft and casual with billowing roses and trailing vines, but there should be an underlying logic to the design and clearly arranged spaces, so guests feel comfortable making their way around outdoors.

In this chapter, you'll find examples of how designers and owners of small outdoor spaces have created entrance gardens that extend a clear and delightful welcome to guests; patios and lawns that are explicit invitations to rest and play; and paths that pull people out of the house to move about and explore the garden.

You'll also find information on creating privacy without filling the garden with shade. As you organize or remodel your own outdoor space (see pages 5–7 for information on where to start), plan for a balance of privacy and openness, shade and sun. It's sunlight, a breeze, and a view of the sky that breathe life into the structure of a garden.

This mini-patio running across the path encourages people to explore the garden at a leisurely pace.

THE ENTRANCE GARDEN

The space between the street and the front door, even if it's only a few yards, is the place to issue a welcome to your guests. If you landscape the area well, people will arrive at your doorstep in a relaxed frame of mind, refreshed, and already delighted by your hospitality.

The most important part of an entrance garden is the path. Make it wide enough for people to arrive comfortably, and mark it well so there is no hesitation about the way to the front door. A path that goes directly to the door is more convenient than one that takes in a tour of the garden; if the path is circuitous, delivery people are likely to forge a shortcut, and guests arriving with a pile of presents will be tempted to take that route, too. Where possible, make the doorstep and the area adjoining it particularly spacious, so there's room for people to linger graciously over good-byes.

Avoid choosing paving that might cause someone to slip or trip or to scuff their shoes. Either poured concrete or cut stone is a good choice, as long as the surface isn't super-smooth because it may be slippery when wet. Gravel can be rough on fine leather shoes, and if it travels indoors (as it always does), it can mar hardwood floors. Fill the gaps between paving with mortar so they don't trap thin heels; plants in the gaps may easily trip someone carrying a package or arriving after dark. Also be mindful of overhanging plants: place prickly plants well away from the walk-

way, and if you want to border the path with romantically flopping lavenders or catmint, make the path very wide, so guests don't have to push through wet foliage after a rain.

Once you've taken care that the path is comfortable, the entrance garden can be anything you want it to be, as long as it doesn't detract from the primary purpose of welcoming people to your house. You might place a table and chairs here if it's the only sunny part of your yard (or, in a hot climate, the only shady part), but keep in mind that a sitting area in an entrance garden—even if it's screened—usually has a more vibrant, public atmosphere than a sitting area secluded in the backyard.

The best entrance gardens are delightful crossings from public space to private space. To help your guests slow down and leave the cares of the world behind as they enter the gate or other garden threshold, decorate the entrance garden elaborately. Plan the plantings so that they are beautiful year-round, and display and maintain them especially well. Dress up the threshold, the front door, and every yard of space between the two to delight the senses.

FACING PAGE: The arching branches of a Japanese snow-drop tree *(Styrax japonicus)* frame a front entrance. As guests make their way to the door through the pools of sunlight flickering on the path, they come upon two chairs that are perhaps used only occasionally but provide a lovely sense of comfort and hospitality. The lively red rhododendron is 'Vulcan'.

Design: Barbara Thompson

Arches of gold flame honeysuckle *(Lonicera heckrottii)* tunnel the view down a long path to the door (left). The journey is made special by the light fragrance and the alternating bands of sunshine and shadow on the floor. If you can arrange it, have the space by the front door be sunny (below); people enjoy walking through shadows toward light.

A picket fence suits a wood-sided house particularly well. Paint it the color of the house and choose post shapes and finials that complement the house style. Stepping the architectural details of the house out to the property line in this way helps settle a large house into the landscape.

Because first impressions do count, ensure plantings in the entrance garden look good all year. The evergreen boxwood balls in this elegant planting design are easily kept neat by regular clipping. The petunias in the pots can be enjoyed at their peak and then replaced with something else. Note the nice detail of the squares of brick paving beneath the pots and the gracious dimensions of the walkway.

Design: Bunny Williams

If you can, start your entrance garden at the easement so the welcome begins there. Plan the planting spaces so that people have room to get out of their cars comfortably, and choose plants that continue the planting scheme near the house. The California poppies *(Eschscholzia californica)* here seem to have escaped the garden boundaries, making a very pleasing natural effect.

Plants in pots set against the wall and mounted on it decorate an entrance garden with little floor space. To minimize maintenance with this many containers, install drip irrigation lines.

Bold red walls carve out a somewhat private area, suggestive of a courtyard, around the path to the door. Note the similarity between the walls' angular lines and the roofline.

Design: Carrie Nimmer

Garden gates are not only for security and privacy. They decorate and play up the threshold, emphasizing the sense of arriving somewhere special. The more care you put into the details of the entrance garden, the greater the sense of hospitality you'll create there.

An evergreen flowering vine makes a fragrant arch over an entranceway in a narrow space. If your front door can't be seen from the street, mark it clearly in a manner such as this so people can find their way in.

This shady entrance garden was made lively and colorful by painting the front door and planting a range of bold hostas beside the path (plants with cream or white blotches and variegations seem to glow in the shade). Note how the chairs match the door and the blue hostas.

THE PATIO AND LAWN

Patios and lawns provide the opportunity to relax outdoors. In designers' small gardens, a large portion of the ground area is usually devoted to these open areas so people can sit with friends as comfortably as if they were indoors, then get up and toss a ball across the grass or stroll about aimlessly in the open air.

A patio next to the house is more convenient than one at the end of the garden path because you can ferry drinks and extra napkins from the kitchen to the outdoor dining table without having to make annoying trips back and forth through the garden. If your garden is too small for permanent outdoor furniture, you can move the kitchen chairs and maybe even the table outside when the occasion calls for it. A patio next to the house also allows for wonderful unplanned moments in the garden: at any time of day, you may be drawn outdoors by the sight of shafts of sunlight warming a comfortable chair.

Patios away from the house are used less often, but they have a magical come-out-to-the-woods attraction and a psychological benefit. Like gazebos and studios settled among the garden trees, they provide a place to go to get away from the busy pace of everyday life. A remote patio, even if it is only 10 yards away from the back door or down a small flight of steps, can be made into a fabulous retreat.

A paved area is more practical than a lawn for outdoor living. Paving wears better than grass and dries out more quickly after a rain, so it's a better surface for frequent foot traffic. You can also erect a ceiling over paving to provide some privacy from the neighbors, whereas grass needs plenty of sunlight to thrive. On the other hand, grass can't be beat for its lush natural look, its softness against bare feet, and its fragrance when mowed. A sward of grass, especially if you let it grow a little long so the breeze riffles through it, brings a sense of the natural landscape into the garden. You can slope a lawn to follow the existing contours of the land or model it into interesting shapes. Grass is also the best surface for play.

In a small garden, it's especially important to put the patio and lawn on the garden plan first, before starting to plant. Once you have the places to sit and dream mapped out well, you can connect them to the house with paths and then screen and decorate them as lavishly as you wish.

FACING PAGE: A floor set into the lawn, so the mower can run over it, provides this outdoor dining area with a firm footing after rain. The odd chair is an asset; people like to have some choice of seating.

Even on a tiny balcony, leave at least a square yard among the plants for a chair in which to sit and enjoy the view. Here that was achieved by elevating the pots onto tiered staging.

A change in paving material, from flagstone near the house to raised wooden decking, sets off the dining area in this small garden. A fountain beyond the deck edge spills sweet music into the space, overriding the sounds of the neighborhood.

Design: Simon Fraser

Patios needn't be large. A patio not much bigger than a lounge chair (above) provides a quiet refuge off a private room in the house and a secret entrance to the garden. A patio can also be just a swelling in the path that allows for a pair of chairs where the view is best or the plants most fragrant (left). In this garden, some patio spaces are open and airy, some intimate and sheltered.

Design (above): Yunghi Epstein

Beds of flowers set into this lawn offer several semiprivate spaces to explore and at the same time maintain an open, flowing atmosphere in the garden. Note how the lawn becomes a path that zigzags into a room marked with a raised urn and then exits at the far side.

For a beautiful sense of shelter combined with an open view, place a seat in front of tall plants or a wall at the lawn's edge. Build a floor and decorate around the seat with bold plants to mark it as a special place (above), or let the flickering light cascading through a katsura tree *(Cercidiphyllum japonicum)* make the place memorable (below).

Design (above): Bill Harris

Design (below): Michael S. Schultz

In an arid climate, paving makes more practical sense than lawn and is more aesthetically appropriate to the natural surroundings. Here, different materials mark different spaces within the courtyard, and interesting objects set in the floor or glimpsed through a breach in the walls draw people out into and through the garden.

Design: Steve Martino

Besides being places for relaxation, patios and lawns provide the open areas from which to study the garden as one piece, to look around and experience the special beauty of the place and see the house in relation to it.

A lawn needn't be flat, and it needn't be all right angles. It can be kidney shaped, divided, and notched (above) to make a bold pattern on the floor and distract the eye from the tight garden boundaries. It can be a classic oval (above right), mounded a little in the center to add interest to the lines. Or it can roll with the terrain (right), emphasizing the natural lay of the land.

Design (above): Randall Speck
Design (above right): Jonathan Baillie
Design (right): Tom Mannion

THE GARDEN PATH

A small garden seems larger if there's a journey through it—a path to take from the back door out to the boundary lines and back. Even in a small urban yard, the journey can feel like an outing into the natural world, away from the sounds and stresses of the city. A balcony can have a path, too; the sight of one invites people to step outside.

To announce that there's something worth seeing on the journey through your garden and to invite people to take the path, mark the path entrance boldly. Flank it with containers, highlight it with a boulder or piece of sculpture, or provide an enticing clue to what lies down the path. Make the space generous here so people can pause to change shoes or mill about and wait for someone to come out from indoors. Think of the path threshold as a trailhead. You might even install a written sign that says "Welcome to my garden" or "This way to the secret garden," but a charming visual scene is more seductive than words. In a very tight place, such as a balcony off the living room, consider dressing up the start of the path with a trailing vine trained over the door or a fountain mounted on the balcony wall.

Next, decide on the path destination. The path should take people somewhere special, such as to a view out of the garden or to a sitting area in the sun. If you can, hide the destination from the beginning of the path so there's a sense of adventure as people set out. If the space is so small the destination can't be hidden, provide some surprise there, such as a fountain bubbling up in a circle of pebbles or a pot of ripe strawberries.

Build up the sense of arrival with more flanking pots, for example, or an arch or a couple of steps, and always provide a comfortable bench or one or two chairs.

Lastly, string out the journey between the start of the path and the destination. Provide as many stopping places as you can: include places to sit that are set back from the path, as well as visual attractions that will make people pause in the journey, such as a view across the garden, reflections in a water bowl, fragrant plantings, or herbs and vegetables to harvest. Make the path seem longer by taking it through different spaces in the garden, from room to room if you like, or simply from a sunny area into shade and back into sun. Mark each new space with a threshold stone (a large slab of cut stone or flagstone), a step up or down, an arch, or a gate. Build subsidiary paths off the main path and decorate the intersection, maybe making it wide enough for a table and chair. On a balcony, perhaps frame different views between screens of vines or hanging plants, so the scenery changes as people walk through the space. The more experiences, or distinct spaces, you can create along the journey, the larger the garden will seem.

FACING PAGE: A path of recycled concrete runs across a hillside, creating a precious level place for exploring the garden and catching views beyond it.

A broad path is more inviting than a narrow one. If you are reluctant to give up planting space, make places for plants in the paving. In the heart of the garden, you can slow people down by making them pick their way around each flower. But in a pathway used after dark, keep the plants low and neat and to the edges of the path so no one trips.

Design: Bob Clark

A path that borders or crosses water is especially beautiful. Place a boulder or a log nearby for watching the reflections of the garden and the movement of the breeze on the water surface. Be sure the edge of the pond or stream is completely firm or the paving will cave in.

Design: Harland Hand

In a garden without formally marked rooms, create distinct spaces by taking a path into a shady area under a tree and back out into the sun. The contrast of light and shade is sensuous and enriches a small garden.

Design: Oehme, van Sweden & Associates

There's often space for a path at the garden boundary. A little screening on either side, such as that provided by the tall alliums and beanpoles here, can turn the path into a private corridor to stroll along, out of sight from the house.

Design: Bunny Williams

A long vista through the garden enlarges it. Look for opportunities to bring a path to a stopping place with a view across the longest part of the garden to a focal point. Frame the view with arches (left) or with architectural plants, such as these pencil-thin conifers (above). If you have a long, narrow garden, emphasize its length by building a path from one edge right to the other (through any intervening rooms).

Steps and arches add interest to a path; their strong lines and hard surfaces emphasize the softness of the surrounding plants. A path also seems longer the more "prepositions" it has: this one (below) goes *up* each step, *past* the pot, *around* the spilling grass stems, *through* the opening, and *into* another part of the garden.

A route through the garden needn't be paved. Cues such as arches and openings between clipped shrubs or potted plants will attract the eye and pull people along from one place to another. In the narrow parts of the route, where there's most wear, pave the floor with a few stepping-stones.

Sitting places draw out the journey through the garden. A low retaining wall (above) makes a space-saving seat when set against a bank of sweet-smelling 'Iceberg' roses and English lavenders and a floor of fragrant thyme. A bench (right) nestled among foliage feels pleasantly sheltered. Except in hot-summer climates, place seats in the sun.

Design (above):
Van Atta Associates

Design (right): Guy Williams

Paths should be compelling. A pool of stones overflowing from the path to the patio (above) puts the path threshold almost at the chairs, enticing people to get up and make their way to the stone fountain. (Note the generous space and flanking containers marking the path threshold.) At the turn in this path (right), the chair catches the eye and pulls people along to that corner, where a view of another stopping place or a beautiful flowering plant at the next turn might draw them on again.

Design (above):
Oehme, van Sweden
& Associates

Just as an entrance garden welcomes people to the house, thresholds within a garden call out the different parts of the space as people walk through. The approach to a garden building—even a shed—can be made into a special place.

Design: Martha Bryan

PRIVACY AND OPENNESS

A garden that has the right amount of privacy allows you to live and work in the garden just as you wish. That may include singing to yourself as you sow seeds or stretching out first thing in the morning on a lounger in the sun, but perhaps also talking to the neighbors occasionally over the low part of the fence.

However privately you wish to live, allow for some amount of openness in the garden to let in the breeze, the sky, and the sun. In some part of the garden, try to leave a view of the city rooftops or a glimpse of neon through the night fog. Even if there's no special view out of the garden, it's pleasant to see the light and feel the air flowing in across the garden boundaries.

So, rather than planting dense, tall screens all around the edges of the garden (which will shrink most gardens to the size of a postage stamp and cover them with deep shade), study where, exactly, you need privacy in your garden. It helps to get very specific and use a scale for the degree of privacy required. For example, give a 10 (for dense screening) to the area around a hot tub, perhaps an 8 to an outdoor sitting area, and a 2 or 3 to a vegetable garden. Consider the seasonal use of each area: for example, perhaps the patio that's away from the house, at the garden boundary, needs screening only in summer because you don't use it very much in the cooler seasons. Perhaps the

vegetable garden needs no screening at all in summer if there's a private place for a chair behind the rows of corn or beans.

For each area of the garden, also consider what you are seeking privacy from. Again, get very specific: which window in the neighbor's house, the actual line of vision, and the likelihood of your privacy being spoiled rather than a remote possibility that it could be.

Privacy solutions can include tree canopies, awnings, umbrellas, potted plants, walls, fences, hedges, gates, pergolas, trellises, or vines. You can choose deciduous plants for light screens in winter, fences that let the light through, hedges with openings cut into them, or walls so low that you can look over them when you're standing and yet eat in privacy when you're seated. Be creative in working out solutions for your garden. Keep in mind that there are several options for every situation in a small garden, and look for the ones that take the least space and let the light in.

FACING PAGE: This quiet corner has a lovely balance of privacy and openness. Note how the light floods through the boundary fence and how the tall, airy white crambe *(Crambe cordifolia)* makes a pretty screen.

Standard roses and other potted plants placed strategically along a balcony railing (above) provide an eye-level screen for this chair in summer, when it's most used, while allowing sunlight to warm the seat and balcony floor.

A wire fence lets light stream through the garden boundary where a solid board fence or wall, for example, would create darkness. Bold elements within the garden, such as these bowling balls and a sculpture by Marcia Donahue, keep the eye from wandering far.

Design: Marcia Donahue

A gazebo (above) or any type of garden room, such as this one made of trellis walls and a beam ceiling (right), is an ideal structure for a private retreat; place one on the garden boundary and screen any of the sides that have poor views with leafy vines or shrubs. Choose the location and the plants to create an enchanting atmosphere: dappled shade is pleasant; deep shade usually isn't.

There are many ways to soften a wall and make it seem less solid, including piercing the wall with a window onto a carefully staged garden scene beyond (left), and painting a trompe l'oeil with a path that extends into the picture from a real path at the base of the wall (above).

Design (left): Bob Clark

Design (above): Fiona Lawrenson

An awning protects the private sitting areas of this terrace from being overlooked from above, and a new potted hedge is beginning to screen the views from neighboring buildings. Note the small table out in the sunshine by the railing, where there's less privacy but a beautiful view. A small space seems larger if it contains contrasting areas of light and shade.

Design: Terence Conran

A garden seems larger when some spaces within it are secluded from others. A sitting area can be hidden behind a clipped hedge (left) or nestled among oakleaf hydrangeas *(Hydrangea quercifolia)* and hostas (above) without losing the feeling of openness.

Design (above): Margaret Atwell

Board fences needn't be flat and monotonous. In this example (left), the variety in board color, height, and width; the gaps between the boards; and the bold dracaena in a decorative pot in front of the fence create great visual interest and a sense of depth. An occasional pocket of color and an intricate arrangement of wood pieces do the same for this solid fence (below).

Design (below): Garrett Eckbo

Even when there's no threat of an intruding gaze, an outdoor living space needs a sense of privacy. An umbrella ceiling and low banks of shrubs and perennials provide a comfortable amount of seclusion for most people.

CREATING A SENSE OF SPACIOUSNESS

Spaciousness is in the eye of the beholder. It can be conjured up in many ways. For example, you might trick the eye to stay away from the garden's tight boundaries and wander in watery reflections of the sky or to skip right over the boundaries to the tops of your neighbor's trees or a distant view of the city or the sea. Multiple destinations within the garden—such as an outdoor dining area, a hide-away, and perhaps a work area where you can while away an hour or two—also make a small garden seem bigger. So do focal points that direct the eye away from the boundary fence to the beautiful elements within the garden.

This chapter explains dozens of ways to create a sense of spaciousness in a small garden. Don't overlook the expansive effect of bringing nature into your yard: lots of birds, butterflies, water, and sunlight evoke the wild landscape. And if you can create a sense of sanctuary—a place to dream and let your imagination run free—no matter how small your garden is, it will feel like a boundless paradise.

A large water bowl filled to the brim reflects the undersides of banana leaves and a bright, spacious view that contains no hints of the garden's boundaries.

Design: Little & Lewis

LOSE THE BOUNDARIES

There are two main ways to make a tight boundary disappear: either hide it, or open it up so the eye goes right to the view beyond. A third way is pure mischief: disorient people with mirrors or overload their senses so the boundary doesn't register (see also "Place Focal Points" on page 36).

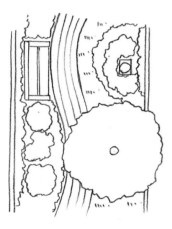

To create a sense of depth in even a very small space, place layers of plants between the boundary and the path and take the plantings from the floor to the sky.

In these two gardens, the boundaries are hidden behind layers of foliage. The tricks are to arrange plants along the garden edge in groups rather than in a line, and to vary the height of the plants from trees to ground covers. Because layering requires a fair amount of garden space, be sure there's room in the center to stroll about in the sun.

Design (above): Oehme, van Sweden & Associates

Design (right): Nancy Hammer Landscape Design

Seize any chance to borrow a neighbor's mature trees as a backdrop for your garden. Settle a rustic retreat against them and tuck woodland plants beneath the canopy to brighten up the shade.

Design (left): Ellen Penick

To direct attention beyond a boundary, edit the views along it, yard by yard, framing and playing up anything of interest, such as a city skyline (above left) or a glimpse of natural water (above). If the boundaries offer no chance of a view out of the garden, make the garden seem larger by occasionally taking the eye straight up to the sky—perhaps by placing a whimsical sculpture on a roof or a balcony (left).

Design (above left): Lee Galen

Sculpture (left): Mark Bulwinkle

Borrowing a view of a neighbor's rural property can greatly add to the apparent size of your small space. As long as you don't invade the other person's privacy, you might make a focal point of that view, with a gate to swing on and watch the horses (below) or an arbor to sit in and gaze over the countryside (right).

Borrow a view of a distant mountain peak or clock tower by aligning the garden axis to it.

A large, open view appears more connected to a small garden and is easier to enjoy when it's presented in panels. Frame portions of it between mounds of grass and shrubs (above) or between trees (left). Playing down the boundary so it's not distracting will also help connect the view to the garden.

Not all boundaries, or all parts of them, need to be hidden. Plain walls, for example, provided they are occasionally interrupted by openings (left), can provide a welcome sense of shelter and make an attractive contrast to plantings. To break up the sense of total enclosure in a courtyard garden, look for opportunities to pierce the wall or to take the eye over a low portion of it or straight up the soaring trunks of palm trees (below).

Design (left): Steve Martino

A concentration of intriguing, bold objects and the heavy fragrance of old roses in the center of this small city garden (below) make it unlikely you'll notice the gray fences on the boundaries.

Design: Frances Butler

A mirror in a window of a garage throws the gaze back from the boundary into the garden.

Design: Sharon Osmond

MAKE TWO SPACES OUT OF ONE

A small garden seems larger if it has a second space within it—a place to explore beyond the area closest to the house. A slight but marked change in grade is one of the easiest ways to create a different garden space. Other options include special paving, hedges, trellises, or a ladder up into the trees.

Brick retaining walls and screens of climbing roses divide an uphill-sloping garden into two levels: a private paved area close to the house and a lawn out in the sun.

Design: Jonathan Baillie

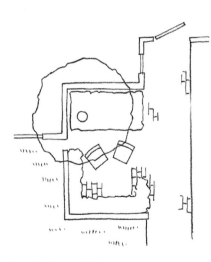

A semiprivate patio bounded by a low stucco wall adds a visually interesting and useful second space to a front yard. The patio lines and materials match those of the house.

A tall trellis creates a private space next to the boundary wall and allows a circular tour of the garden. The planters along the straight section of the path separate it from the return loop.

Design: Duane Paul Design Team

A raised deck creates a comfortable, level outdoor living space in a garden that slopes away from the house. The graciously wide steps are an invitation to leave the deck and explore the garden proper.

A small area of brick paving, with a chair and a couple of pots, makes a patio between a bedroom and the garden. The floor is clean and comfortable enough to bare feet that people can step in and out of the house without thinking.

Design: Dan Borroff Landscape

Call attention to the different areas of the garden by clearly marking the thresholds. An arch like this one (top) is a simple option; even when the vine is not in bloom, the arch frame and the change in paving are excellent visual cues that you are crossing into a different space. A gate, especially through a tall hedge (bottom), marks a threshold most dramatically.

A hedge, trellis, or fence is often used to mark off one area of a garden from another. To avoid creating shady, cramped-looking areas, keep the boundaries as open or low as possible. And seize any chance to make them fun.

Design: Ron Simple

A single freestanding pillar and an overhead create an extra room in a corner of a small garden. Raised beds provide a separate area for the plantings, display the plants closer to eye level, offer seating on the bed edges, and reduce the dominating effect of the tall boundary walls.

Design: Maggie Judycki

A change in flooring alone can distinguish an outdoor dining space if the paving is sufficiently bold. For a pleasant sense of enclosure, place the table close to a wall (left) or make a partial wall with trellises (above).

Design (left): Oehme, van Sweden & Associates

Design (above): Kristina Fitzsimmons

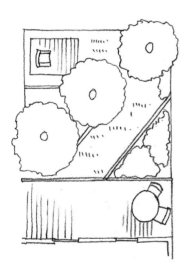

The two decks in this garden are separated by a lawn path that runs on the diagonal, which puts more distance between them than a direct, straight path would.

Just for the fun of it, consider marking out playful spaces in the garden, with, for example, this ring of gazing balls mounted on poles.

A children's garden on a terrace (left) provides many different spaces and opportunities for different activities —a sandy "beach" where the furniture is, a painted ocean between the beach and the skyline, easily movable tables for writing and dining, container plants for gardening, and objects to play with and touch, as well as areas of sun and shade. Terraces designed for adults (right) also need a range of interesting spaces and things to do—different places to sit but also places to walk and smell the flowers or catch a view.

Design (left): Topher Delaney
Design (right): Rob Barnett

Garden buildings or shelters can provide a second place to explore. This wooden shed (below) in a Japanese-style contemplation garden has been made interesting with a wall sculpture, dark paintwork, and a paper lantern glowing in the window. The most exciting extra space you can build in a garden is perhaps a tree house (right): the world in the tree-tops seems a thousand miles away from the world on the ground. Make it accessible for adults as well as children.

Design (right): Ron Wagoner, Nani Waddoups

PLACE FOCAL POINTS

Focal points draw the eye or point the direction to the beautiful elements of the garden, keeping attention away from tight boundaries or undesirable views. To make your garden look bigger, place one focal point at the end of the longest vista you can devise and hide others to create surprises throughout the garden.

People are drawn to water; it's a natural focal point. At this raised pond (above), hidden in a small, private area of the garden, a person can sit on the pond edge and while away an hour. Water in a large bowl sited out in the open (left), as a focal point to an herb garden, provides a compelling place for the eye to rest.

Design (above): Ben Caldwell

Design (left): Stephanie Kotin and Christopher Tebbutt, Land & Place

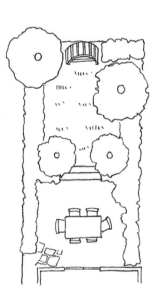

A focal point, such as an arch, at the end of the garden emphasizes the garden's length.

The dramatically shaped leaves of these gunnera make a bold focal point, and the simple green background sets them off perfectly. Focal points placed against fussy or very colorful backgrounds lose their impact.

Design: Marietta O'Byrne

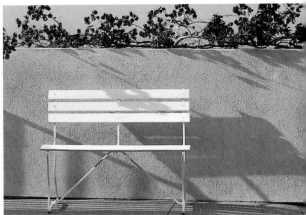

Garden furniture should be not only comfortable but also handsome to look at as part of the view. A bench by a courtyard wall patterned with shadows (above) or two chairs at the end of a garden path (left) will take the eye, and then surely the feet, out into the garden.

Design (above): Isabelle Greene and Associates

Placing a patio away from the house but still visible from it creates a sure focal point in the garden. Note the simple decorative elements: the sculptural shape of the patio tree, the pleasingly crafted stone walls, and the gleam of water spilling over rock.

Design: Oehme, van Sweden & Associates

Decorative objects can lead the eye to a focal point or help ground a view. A large urn (far left), raised on a brick plinth to make it taller and give it more presence, pulls attention to a white wisteria tree. An obelisk (left) provides a place for the eye to settle among a sweep of lily-of-the-Nile *(Agapanthus)*; without it, the garden would be just a foreground to the distant view.

A classical sundial adds interest and delight to a stroll around a small garden. It is a particularly useful decoration when the plants are not in bloom.

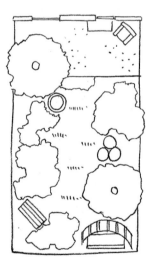

Focal points off the grass garden path—a water bowl, a group of containers, a bench, and an arbor—surprise and enchant people as they walk through the space.

Plants with variegated leaves, such as striped grasses, or with bold flowers, such as cannas, can be used to catch the eye and pull people through a garden—on to the corner of a path (left) or straight to the boundary wall (above). Repeating a striking plant, such as these potted aloes (right), sets up a series of visual cues that people will follow around the garden.

Design (left): Marcia Donahue

Design (above): Linda Cochran

Design (right): Tim Curry

Although most focal points are set up to be seen from the house, the main patio, or the start of a path, don't forget the view back from the bottom of the garden. The house may make a fine focal point; it's always pleasant to see it settled into the garden.

INVITE NATURE IN

Birds, butterflies, breezes, and seasons pay no attention to the garden's boundaries and remind us of wild landscapes. Reflections of clouds, and plants reseeding so prolifically they seem to be roaming free, also expand the sense of space in a small garden.

A corner planting for hummingbirds is full of vivid red and blue nectar-producing flowers.

HUMMINGBIRD GARDEN

A. *Lonicera periclymenum* 'Serotina'. Woodbine

B. *Salvia × superba* 'Blue Hill'

C. *Penstemon barbatus* 'Prairie Fire'

D. *Alcea rosea (Althaea rosea)*. Hollyhock

E. *Salvia splendens,* dwarf red strain. Scarlet sage

F. *Asclepias tuberosa,* yellow cultivar. Butterfly weed

G. *Heuchera sanguinea.* Coral bells

H. *Petunia × hybrida,* blue or purple

I. *Lychnis chalcedonica.* Maltese cross

J. *Agastache foeniculum.* Anise hyssop

K. *Nicotiana alata,* Nicki strain, mixed colors. Flowering tobacco

L. *Digitalis × mertonensis.* Foxglove

FACING PAGE: Wrens, bluebirds, and chickadees are among the birds that may shelter and nest in birdhouses if there's a shortage of natural woodland in the vicinity. Not all types of birds will nest in the same kind of house, so before you buy a house or start to build one, consult a reference such as Sunset's *Attracting Birds.* Birds also need food such as berries and seeds, and water for drinking and bathing.

Place a chair in a butterfly garden so that when it's warm enough for the butterflies to fly (usually at least 60°F/16°C), you can watch the changing iridescent colors on their wings and their lilting or darting patterns of flight up close. To encourage butterflies to stay in your garden, provide a hibernation spot, such as a woodpile, and the favorite host plant for the larvae to feed on. For a simple butterfly garden, see page 42. For more plants that attract butterflies, see page 111.

This large, water-filled metal container surrounded with sedum (top) attracts birds and butterflies and reflects the movement of clouds and changes in the weather and seasons. Also, like a spring or a well, it reminds us that water is the source of all life in the natural world. A

fountain (above) adds the relaxing sound of falling water; the sound is prettiest if the water spills, splashes, and drips from one stone surface to another rather than drops in one simple fall. Fish (right) flashing through a pond draw the eye into the mysterious world below the water surface, to the sheltered places under the lily leaves and the shadows on the silty floor.

Design (middle): Pamela Woods

BUTTERFLY GARDEN

A. *Asclepias tuberosa.*
Butterfly weed

B. *Solidago virgaurea*
'Goldenmosa'.
Goldenrod

C. *Agastache foeniculum.*
Anise hyssop

D. *Spiraea japonica*
'Anthony Waterer'

E. *Liatris spicata.*
Gayfeather

F. *Echinacea purpurea*
'Magnus'.
Purple coneflower

G. *Aster × frikartii* 'Mönch'

H. *Achillea taygetea*

I. *Nepeta × faassenii.*
Catmint

A sense of natural abundance or nature run wild is a precious quality in a small garden. Let nature take over a woodpile (above left), or make it look as if that's what happened. Consider planting a few reseeding annuals or perennials that will jump boundaries and come up under your feet (above), or growing trees that fruit way over your head (right).

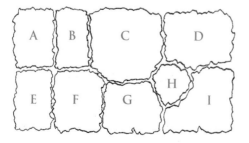

A small border of colorful, nectar-producing flowers attracts butterflies throughout the bloom season, from late spring into fall.

Be sure your garden includes plants that remind you of the changing seasons. The sight of delicate bulbs in fresh spring air, roses at midsummer, buff grasses and dark seed heads in fall, or bright berries in the first winter snow instantly releases the mind from the constraints of small spaces. Place fragrant plants along the garden path or close to doorways and seats.

Design (right): Annie Huntinton

A pleasant breeze that comes in from the fields or the ocean is refreshing and sets the treetops in motion, but on a rooftop too much breeziness is a major obstacle to outdoor living. Instead of a complex array of windbreaks around sitting areas, the designer of this rooftop space on a San Francisco skyscraper (left) chose colorful windsocks and a thrilling display of the site's weather and city view. In more protected gardens, place bamboos or grasses, which whisper and creak beautifully in the wind, where they'll catch an occasional breeze —a strong wind rustles them too roughly. These stalks of giant Chinese silver grass *(Miscanthus giganteus)* record even the slightest breeze (below).

Design (left): Topher Delaney

CATCH THE LIGHT

Small gardens, usually partially shaded by buildings and privacy screens, need cheerful places where sunlight streams through the foliage and pools on the garden furniture, the flowers, and the floor. Study how the light falls in your garden and devise as many opportunities as you can to make the garden sparkle.

Still water in a pool (above) or a simple, wide-rimmed pot (right) catches bright reflections of the light in the sky, even when the water is in shadow. Place tall fountain jets (below) in full sun, so the streams of water will glitter with reflected light.

Design (above): Oehme, van Sweden & Associates

Design (right): Little & Lewis

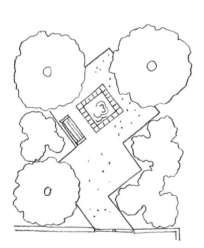

Make a large clearing between the garden plantings to catch the light. Place a still pond or water bowl there to reflect the sky.

Plants with interesting silhouettes and foliage shapes are beautiful when placed where the sun will illuminate them from behind (left). Trees such as these Japanese maples *(Acer palmatum)* reveal the exquisite lines of their branches and the filminess of their leaves (below).

Design (left): Ben Caldwell

Sunlight replicates the pattern of the fence and the shapes of the wisteria flowers on a plain wooden floor (below). The show changes as the light moves and fades, and whenever a breeze shifts the flowers. Note the spacing between the arbor rafters; wide gaps ensure that light travels through the arbor roof.

A hole in a wall provides a shady area with an enchanting view into a light-filled part of the garden. Fences, hedges, and screens can be pierced in the same way; the hole needn't be large enough for a person to stride through.

Design: Gordon Riggle

A wall can be decorated with sculpture, plant pots, or a vine, but check first whether it might best be left bare, to capture the delicate, moving images of a tree.

Paving and simple ground covers such as moss (below) and lawn (right) make fine surfaces for catching the play of light in the garden. Note that the shadows on green surfaces are deep emerald—prettier than the dun shadows on paving.

Design (right): Oehme, van Sweden & Associates

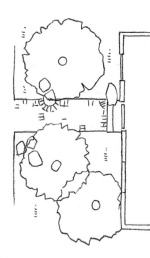

To bring light into an entrance garden shaded by trees, thin the canopies and limb up the trunks (see page 91). Draw attention to the brightness by placing groups of boulders where the sunlight dapples the garden floor.

All reflective surfaces—such as mirrors, gazing balls, and these glass balls—catch the light. Consider placing a few shiny ornaments in shady areas to bring light there.

Design: Sharon Osmond

In fall, the low light warms these ornamental grasses. A pot of bright chrysanthemums ensures you turn your attention this way.

Cream- or white-variegated leaves (above left and above) lighten up the shady parts of a garden. Chartreuse or gold foliage also has a bright, warming effect in shade. For cloudy seasons and twilight parties outdoors, plant white or blue flowers (left); they glow in poor light.

Design (above): Florence Everts

CREATE A SANCTUARY

A garden that is or includes a cherished refuge from the cares of everyday life never feels small. To achieve a sense of sanctuary, build sheltered spaces and furnish your garden so it is a place to relax and dream.

Even a small city garden sometimes has a narrow strip long enough for a lap pool. If that's your idea of heaven, at least inquire about its feasibility. Use a dark plaster for the interior so the bottom of the pool disappears from view and the water surface dances with bright reflections.

A tree and tall, vine-covered screens provide privacy for a hot tub off a bedroom.

A miniature landscape, such as this one created with boulders placed on an island of moss in an expanse of raked gravel (above), can draw the eye away from the immediate surroundings and into a seemingly vast landscape of rocky cliffs, lush green fields, and an endless sea. Choose stable-looking boulders with simple shapes, and a ground cover with a tiny scale. A maze— even this little circle of stones on the floor (right)—provides another interesting journey in a small space.

Design (right): Ivan Hicks

A sanctuary requires a strong sense of shelter, which can be achieved in several ways. Consider creating a secluded or sunken garden within tall double hedges (above), placing a gazebo against trees and covering the roof with vines (left), or simply installing a chair among tall plants (right). Still water makes an excellent ornament for a sanctuary because it helps quiet the mind.

Design (above): Bunny Williams

Design (right): Edith Edelman

This outdoor room (below), with a leafy ceiling, a hearth with a sofa and a chair drawn up to it, and tree shadows playing with the smoke on the walls, is an idyllic sanctuary at all times of day and in many kinds of weather.

In dark, hidden places, such as this shaded room under a weeping willow (above left) and this city garden below street level (above), other worlds can be created that are refreshingly different from the world out in the open. The ruins under the willow are inhabited by stone monkeys. Fashion designer Zandra Rhodes filled her tiny basement garden with exotic carvings, making it look like a ruined religious site.

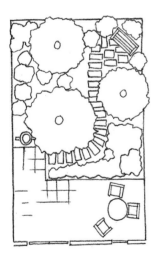

A bench set back and sheltered among tall shrubs at the end of the garden, out of view from the house, makes a simple sanctuary.

A tree in the side yard provides privacy and shelter for a bench against the house wall. Imagine how the light changes as a breeze stirs the blossom-laden branches. The privacy afforded by a tree can be magical; just be sure some light travels through the canopy when it's in full leaf.

Home should look like a sanctuary. Soften the architecture with plants so that every return to the house is pleasurable and comforting.

A personally significant statue can lift you out of a worrying frame of mind by reminding you of the beauty and preciousness of life.

Design: Stephanie Kotin and Christopher Tebbutt, Land & Place

Sometimes, placing garden elements so they're discovered almost by accident is what embues them with a sense of peace. Quiet water that is hidden and almost inaccessible (left) has a powerful aura of stillness, as does this fanciful castle in the shelter of a pretty bank and a giant hosta (below).

Design (left): Harland Hand

DECORATE WITHOUT ORNAMENTS

More than one or two cute garden ornaments can make a small garden look fussy. Instead of purchasing decorative objects, consider the many ways you can make the functional elements of the garden visually interesting.

Hedges needn't be plain. A hedge of apples pruned into a candelabra espalier (above) makes an ornamental boundary. A solid hedge (right) may combine several different hedge plants, and the top may be stepped up and down.

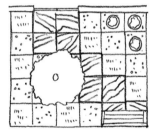

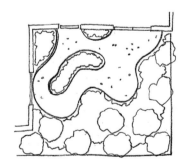

A strong ground pattern delights the eye. It is especially effective when seen from a terrace or window overlooking the garden. At top, squares of slate set into a floor of grass and pebbles lead to a bench. At bottom, a sinuous gravel path loops around an island bed.

Low boxwood hedges run joyous loops around this flower garden; the lines are pleasing even when the plants are not in bloom.

Paint on the doors and eaves of a shed or the poles of an arbor or plant support can bring a garden to life, especially if you choose vivid contrasting colors, such as yellow and purple (below). Consider also using paint on a plain old gate to the vegetable garden (right) to turn it into something playful and memorable or on plain pots (below right) to highlight the colors of a foliage plant (see pages 80–81).

Design (below): Bob Dash

Fences come in many decorative styles. A fancy white picket with round caps on the posts creates a hospitable impression at a house entrance.

Design: Greg Trutza

DESIGN SIMPLE PLANTINGS

In a small space, it's tempting to squeeze in as many different plants as you can, but variety without a sense of order is irritating—the eye becomes restless and moves over the garden quickly. By contrast, simple plantings and carefully arranged ones are satisfying and easy on the eye. They encourage slow appreciation and make a garden seem larger.

A simple order reigns among these diverse plants: the colors were chosen to work with the colors of the house. Some of the flower and leaf colors exactly match the wall and trim colors; the others contrast with them to make a lively effect.

Design: Bob Moore

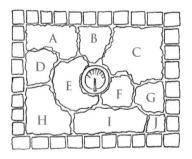

A geometric shape and a central sundial bring a sense of order and simplicity to this collection of different herbs.

HERB GARDEN

A. *Origanum vulgare.*
Oregano

B. *Rosa* 'Sunsprite'

C. *Rosmarinus officinalis.*
Rosemary

D. *Origanum majorana (Majorana hortensis).*
Sweet marjoram

E. *Santolina chamaecyparissus* 'Nana'.
Lavender cotton

F. *Artemisia dracunculus.*
French tarragon

G. *Allium schoenoprasum.*
Chives

H. *Salvia officinalis* 'Icterina'.
Common sage

I. *Nepeta × faassenii.*
Catmint

J. *Thymus × citriodorus* 'Aureus'.
Lemon thyme

Repeating plants along a border sets up a rhythm that is pleasing to the eye. If the plantings here were fussy, guests might turn away from the path or walk it quickly.

Design: Joanna Reed

A mass of poppies makes a big splash of color that stands out in a small space. The slight color variations and spreading growth pattern remind one of wildflower meadows.

Design: Carrie Nimmer

Gardens that are predominantly green are usually peaceful, refreshing places. Use touches of flower color, such as these spring dogwood and allium blossoms, to mark the seasons.

Design: Oehme, van Sweden & Associates

Groups of accent plants, such as these ligularia (left), can create a delightfully extravagant effect in a modest space. The show is bolder, more eye-catching, and more exciting than a hodgepodge of different plants competing for attention. It's also easy to achieve and maintain.

Harmonious colors are the easiest to gaze at. Choose colors that sit next to one another on the color wheel, such as cool purple and warm pink, yellow and chartreuse, orange and gold, or blue and violet.

HIDE YOUR STUFF

Tools, extra pots, and children's playthings can ruin the look of a small garden unless they're hidden or displayed well. Be careful about what you buy. Be creative about transforming what you have.

Bright-colored plastic play structures are hard to hide or settle into a small garden. A playhouse in the treetops (above) or a bowl of water doing double duty as a water garden (right) might be just as entertaining for a child (see information on water safety, page 85).

Design (above and right): Lawson, Carter, Epstein

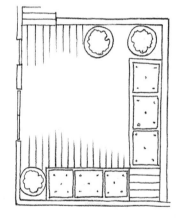

Built-in benches on a deck have hinged seats with storage space beneath.

The cycle of life and death is at the very heart of the garden. A tidy, well-turned compost pile that's as unobtrusive as this one is a pleasant way to reveal it.

A garden shed needn't be unsightly or dull. Make it interesting by planting houseleeks *(Semper-vivum)* on the roof, installing a mirror window to reflect the trees and sky, and planting a little garden in front to partially screen it.

Garden tools and equipment can be quite attractive and the shed a worthy garden destination. Keep things clean and arrange them so visitors can comfortably stop for a while to look through old seed catalogs, check the temperature, or inspect a collection of pots or your apple harvest.

MAKING THE MOST OF
SMALL SPACES

An ideal garden has somewhere to sit, privacy, places to plant flowers and vegetables, and visual delights such as a reflection pool and an arch smothered with roses. You don't have to sacrifice any of these elements in a small garden. Rather, the trick is to put your imagination to work in making the most of the space you have.

In this chapter, you'll find ideas for expanding the planting and decorative opportunities within every inch of the garden, including the walls and fences and even the treetops. You'll also find information on choosing comfortable furniture for small spaces, building and growing screens to help you gain privacy without barricading yourself in, and salvaging an inherited jungle to reclaim some sunlight.

As you start your garden plan, check out the "Double Features" section on page 88. In the best small gardens, every element has at least two uses. For example, a wall fountain can decorate a dull wall, make a focal point to the view from the sitting area, and replace the drone of traffic with the pleasant sounds of water splashing against stone.

Every step along the path of this city garden reveals something exquisite to stop and look at.
Design: Sharon Osmond

SITTING AREAS

The ultimate outdoor sitting area has every comfort—sun and shade, warmth, privacy, a view, shelter from wind, cozy furniture, and candlelight and firelight after dark.

FINDING A PERFECT SITE

When trying to decide where to locate an outdoor sitting area, look for a site that is warm and sheltered from the wind, enclosed enough to feel intimate and private, and yet open to a view, either out of the garden or to an interesting feature within it. If you have lived with your garden for a while, you'll know your favorite places; they may have one or more of these characteristics. Investigate those locations first as possible sitting areas.

A sitting area adjoining the house is convenient because you can easily transport iced drinks and cushions to and fro. But a patio away from the house offers a restful place to go to get away from the telephone and everyday chores. The fact that you have to go some distance to it—even if it's just around a corner—makes the garden feel larger. Consider having both kinds of sitting areas. Perhaps there's space off the master bedroom or bathroom that is large enough for a chair and gets morning light, or a corner in the garden where there's a lovely view of the sun setting over someone else's trees. Explore the side yard, the front yard, and the backyard for possibilities.

Before you make a final choice, check the area for wind. Many factors, including neighboring buildings and fences, affect the movement of air. Post small flags or ribbons in the area and note their movements during windy periods. If you need shelter, choose a somewhat permeable barrier over a solid one (see "No Shelter from Wind" on page 94).

Once you've decided on a spot, you can make the space more defined and roomlike by growing a low hedge wall, setting an arch at the entrance or tall potted plants around the perimeter, or erecting screens. Alternatively, if you don't want to enclose the sitting area too much, provide just a "ceiling" by building an arbor, planting a small tree with a broad canopy, or installing a garden umbrella by your chair. A ceiling will define the sitting area, as well as block views from above.

SUN VERSUS SHADE

The best sitting areas have both sun and shade. In those situations, people have the option of seating themselves where the light suits them. But if you have to choose either one or the other, generally a sunny location is better. There are several ways to provide shade if the sun becomes too bright—with an arbor, an umbrella, a tree canopy, or an awning, for example—and fewer ways to prevent a shady patio from seeming gloomy.

The south side of the house, in the path of the sun for most of the day, is warmest; the west side, which gets afternoon sun, is next warmest, followed by the east side, which receives morning sun. The north side is the coldest place because it's shaded almost all day. Consider which times of the day you'll want to sit outdoors, and observe the sun patterns in your garden. If a northern exposure is your only choice in a cool climate, try to extend the sitting area away from the house walls so that at least a part of it is in sunlight.

CHOOSING FURNITURE

One good way to narrow the dauntingly vast field of available garden furniture is first to consider the location and style of your garden. For a patio off the house, match the material to the style of the indoor furniture and choose something as well crafted. For a rustic part of the garden, choose country materials, such as wood or willow, or forget conventional furniture and use logs and flat-topped boulders.

Metal furniture used to mean Victorian-looking, cast-iron benches that were cold and uncomfortable to sit on and too heavy to move. Nowadays, you can buy wrought-iron furniture with metal mesh seats that have more give; cast aluminum or steel furniture that looks like heavy metal but is lightweight; and lightweight enameled or powder-coated, aluminum-frame furniture that won't rust. Metal furniture also now suits either contemporary or traditional garden styles.

Wood furniture is natural-looking, and it ages gracefully. Teak and redwood are favored choices because of their beauty, strength, and resistance to insects and rot. (To avoid depleting natural supplies, purchase only plantation-grown teak or recycled redwood.) Wood that needs painting or staining to preserve it can be colored to match the house or garden colors, but avoid white because it causes too much glare in strong sunlight.

Furniture made of wicker or rattan is comfortable because it has a natural flexibility, but the real thing is not durable enough to last outside a covered porch. Synthetic wicker is undaunted by weather.

Canvas directors' chairs and deck chairs are particularly useful for a small space. They are more comfortable than folding French bistro furniture, portable, fairly tough, easily stored, inexpensive, and available in a wide range of fabric colors.

Be sure to check the comfortableness of chairs before you purchase them; some garden furniture is not sufficiently comfortable for leisurely outdoor living. Also determine how much maintenance the furniture needs, if any; how durable it is in wet winters and whether it must be covered or stored indoors; whether the chairs and tables fold or stack; how easy the furniture is to move; exactly how much space it occupies (do the chairs slide under the table when not in use?); and whether it'll stand firm or wobble on your sitting area floor (chairs with small feet may get stuck in the joints between paving units).

ALLOCATING SPACE FOR FURNITURE

Furniture takes up a lot of space in the garden. It's easy to underestimate just how much space, so before you buy, get the dimensions of the pieces and mark them out on your patio or garden floor with construction chalk. Visualize these marks as solid objects and leave plenty of space for people to walk around them. Factor in room for plants, for serving or side tables, or for a barbecue, if you're planning one.

To save space, build in seating wherever there's an opportunity. For example, put benches into a deck rail, cap a low wall or raised bed with planks wide enough to sit on or place food trays on, and make garden steps wide enough for seating. A cheap folding table is useful if you have no space for a permanent table; store it in the garage and put a pretty cloth over it when you need it for the garden.

MOOD LIGHTING

Candles set in glass jars send flickering pools of warm, soft light into the shadows at twilight. Standard electric lighting designed for gardens never quite matches the effect, even if it's shielded and turned low, but a chandelier rigged up just for the night provides a great sense of occasion.

Firelight also has a convivial effect; people stay late if there's a chance to sit under the stars and gaze into a fire. If you don't want to go to the expense of building a fireplace, consider buying a brazier or a small, freestanding clay chimney with a built-in fire bowl (a *chimenea*).

CLEARANCE AROUND SEATS

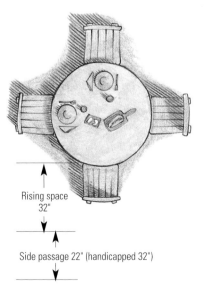

Rising space
32"

Side passage 22" (handicapped 32")

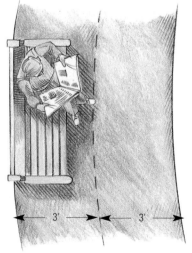

3'   3'

ARBORS

In a small garden, an arbor can provide some privacy or define an outdoor living area. A simple one is within the reach of most do-it-yourselfers, with the help of a friend or two to raise the beams into place. If you know how to use a router, you can make decorative details on the beams and round the edges of the posts. If you don't want to use even a saw, look for prefabricated arbors available from many nurseries and mail-order suppliers.

DESIGN OPTIONS

An arbor consists of posts or columns topped by horizontal beams, which in turn support rafters and lath. An arbor can be freestanding or attached to the house. In the latter case, a "ledger" (usually a 2 by 4 or 2 by 6) secured to the house wall supports the rafters on one side, rather than posts and a beam.

There are numerous choices of materials for posts, beams, and rafters. A formal arbor might have a decorative white wooden roof supported on elegant stone columns, a rustic grape arbor might be made of pressure-treated poles and beams with wires instead of rafters, and a southwestern ramada-style arbor might incorporate mesquite poles and ocotillo stems.

To filter the light or to screen the inside of the arbor from an uphill neighbor, grow vines over the rafters (deciduous ones for the most light in winter) or cover the rafters with lath, lattice, poles, woven reeds, bamboo, or tree or grape stakes. The wider the material and the closer the spacing, the more shade it will provide; a tight latticework grid, for example, will provide more shade than thin lath. The direction in which you lay lath or poles will also affect how much shade they cast at different times of the day (for midday shade, run the lath east-west; for more shade in the morning and early evening, run it north-south). If you want to cover the arbor with a vine, you can train it directly over the rafters; don't lay lath or poles across the rafters first or you may create too much shade.

Match the size of the arbor to the scale of the surrounding architecture and the purpose for which you'll use it. If you plan to place an outdoor dining table under the arbor, allow at least 4½ feet of clearance all around the table for people to take their seats comfortably and additional room for a barbecue or a table to place a tray. As you make the calculations, allow for the space any vines on the posts will need. The more room there is under the arbor, the more gracious the space will feel. The arbor should also be tall. The height of an interior door is 6 feet 8 inches, so the arbor should be at least that tall; most are much taller to allow room for vines and to suit the grander scale of the outdoors.

CONSTRUCTION POINTERS

Before you set a single post, check with your local building department for regulations affecting the construction of arbors. In many communities, you will have to meet building codes and obtain a permit before you begin work.

For the longest-lasting posts, beams, and rafters, choose only pressure-treated wood or naturally decay-resistant materials, such as redwood or cedar heartwood. You can use 4-by-4 posts for most arbors up to 12 feet tall. What size beams to use depends on the distance between the posts and the distance between beams; rafter size is based on beam spacing. For more information on beam and rafter sizes, see Sunset's *Trellises and Arbors.*

Posts are set in concrete footings, typically 1 foot square and 8 inches deep. If you're planning to set your posts in lawn or dirt, you'll need to raise them above ground level to prevent standing water from

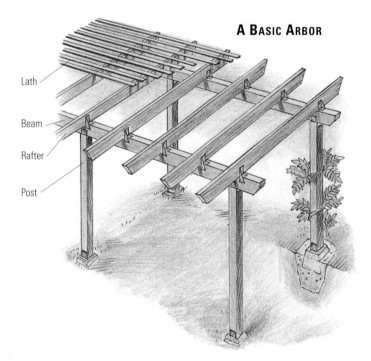

A BASIC ARBOR

Lath

Beam

Rafter

Post

rotting the posts. The easiest way to do that is to set precast concrete piers into the footings (see facing page) and then nail the posts into the piers' cast-in metal anchors.

If your arbor will span an existing patio, you can position the footings outside the edge of the patio or break through the existing paving, dig holes, and pour new footings. If you're planning to install a new concrete patio, you can pour the footings and the slab at the same time. Use metal anchors (shown below) or concrete piers with cast-in anchors to connect the posts to the concrete slab.

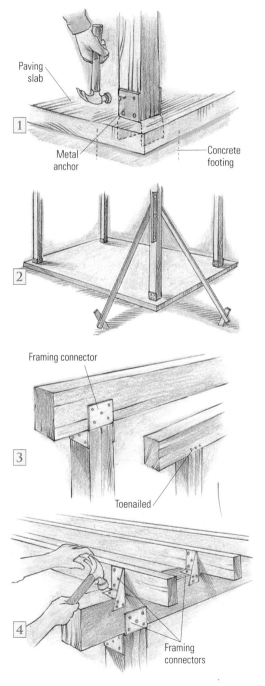

Paving slab

1

Metal anchor

Concrete footing

Framing connector

3

Toenailed

4

Framing connectors

BUILDING AN ARBOR

1 Precut the posts to length. Set the posts in metal anchors embedded in concrete footings or atop precast piers. Hold each post vertical and nail the anchor to it.

2 Check that each post is vertical by plumbing it with a level on two adjacent sides. Secure in position with temporary braces nailed to wooden stakes that are driven into the ground.

3 With a helper, position a beam on top of the posts. Check that the posts are still vertical and the beam is level (adjust if necessary with shims); then secure the beam to the posts with framing connectors or by toenailing it to the posts (shown at left). Repeat for remaining beams.

4 Set and space the rafters on top of the beams and secure them with framing connectors or by toenailing them. For extra strength, you can install diagonal bracing between the posts and beams. For shade, cover the rafters with vines or lath, either 1 by 2s or 2 by 2s. Space the lath as necessary to achieve a specific amount of shade.

ROOM WITH VIEWS

A gazebo, with its walls and solid roof, offers more seclusion than a plain overhead and more shelter from the weather. The ideal location is at the bottom of the garden, in a leafy, quiet place. Plant vines or tall shrubs to block any unsightly views from the gazebo's windows, but leave open any pleasant ones across the garden and back toward the house. If you can't conceal the gazebo, choose a style that matches the house architecture. Some models come with built-in seats, but they're not always comfortable to sit on. For a gracious tea party on roomy wicker chairs, you'll need a gazebo with plenty of floor space.

LIVING GREEN SCREENS

Screens of hedges and vines define garden boundaries and are easier and less expensive to make than fences or walls. They contribute a lush look to a small space; they can be clipped into pleasing shapes or left to grow loose and wild; and they change with the seasons, producing a flush of spring flowers or a topping of brilliant green new growth.

CREATING PRIVACY WITH PLANTS

Screens have two main uses in the garden: to create a boundary on the property line and to separate areas within the garden. The garden example below shows different ways plants can be used to create screens.

Before you begin planting boundary screens, think about your neighbors. Don't plant trees or shrubs that will eventually outgrow their spaces or extend too far into neighbors' yards or rob them of sunlight. Check local ordinances, restrictions, and easements that could affect your plans. Many communities have guidelines that protect solar access or beautiful views.

CHOOSING A HEDGE PLANT

A mature hedge can vary in height from 1 foot tall to as high as you can trim it from the top of a ladder (or scaffolding). Are you looking for a low edge to a flower bed, a hedge about chest high to define an outdoor dining area, or a tall hedge for maximum privacy? The list of suggested hedging plants on page 105 contains information on hedge size and growth pattern to help you create a suitable border.

Before you zero in on fast-growing plants, consider the extra maintenance they require. Fast-growing hedges grown in a formal or semiformal style (see facing page) need almost constant clipping. Large, very fast growing hedging plants, such as Leyland cypress *(Cupressocyparis leylandii)*, can quickly get away from you in a small garden. Instead, choose plants with more moderate growth and, if you like, fill in the gaps around them for the first two years with tall, quick-growing annuals and perennials, such as foxgloves or cosmos.

Evergreen shrubs are the standard choice for hedges. They make plain backdrops for the decorative elements of the garden, and if you use the same plants for most of your screening, they will unify the garden and give it great structure. Where privacy is not a particular concern during winter, you might plant a deciduous hedge with fine flowers or fall foliage as a garden accent, or perhaps plant a double hedge, with the decorative one backed by a taller, fine-textured evergreen one. The deciduous hedge's flowers or fall foliage will stand out beautifully against it. Hornbeam and beech hedges are popular deciduous hedges because they hold onto their dry russet leaves well into winter.

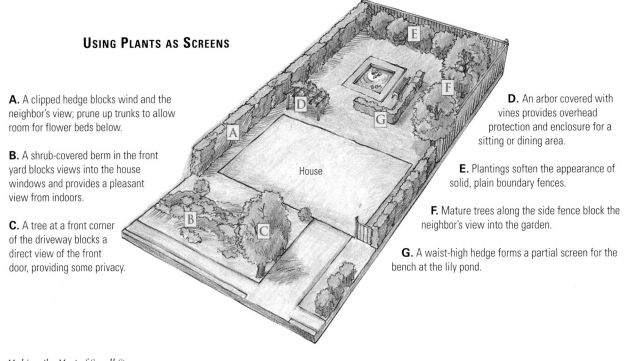

USING PLANTS AS SCREENS

A. A clipped hedge blocks wind and the neighbor's view; prune up trunks to allow room for flower beds below.

B. A shrub-covered berm in the front yard blocks views into the house windows and provides a pleasant view from indoors.

C. A tree at a front corner of the driveway blocks a direct view of the front door, providing some privacy.

House

D. An arbor covered with vines provides overhead protection and enclosure for a sitting or dining area.

E. Plantings soften the appearance of solid, plain boundary fences.

F. Mature trees along the side fence block the neighbor's view into the garden.

G. A waist-high hedge forms a partial screen for the bench at the lily pond.

FORMAL AND SEMIFORMAL HEDGES

A formal hedge presents itself as a single unit with a smooth, sheared top and sides. You can clip it so that it's boxy, rounded, or pointy topped; in cold climates where snow load can distort the shape of hedges, a round or pointed top will help shed snow. Because their growth is so restricted, formal hedges usually take up less space than semiformal or informal hedges. Their growth is also denser; some formal hedges are almost as impenetrable as a wall.

The best plants for formal hedging are rugged small-leafed types, such as boxwood, yew *(Taxus),* hemlock *(Tsuga),* and arborvitae *(Platycladus* and *Thuja),* which are grown for their foliage rather than flowers or fruit. Their neat, fine-textured appearance makes a handsome backdrop to foreground plantings of flowers, and light and shadows play across their surfaces beautifully.

A semiformal hedge appears as a single unit, too, but the overall effect is softer, looser, and more billowy. This style is especially suitable for large-leafed plants, such as English laurel *(Prunus laurocerasus),* which would get chopped and disfigured by close clipping for a formal hedge. Plants chosen for their flowers or fruit, such as myrtle *(Myrtus communis)* or holly *(Ilex),* will provide a better show in a semiformal hedge than in a formal one because you can prune to preserve some of the flower buds.

INFORMAL HEDGES

For an informal hedge, you let the shrubs assume their natural shape, treating them just like individual plants that happen to be growing in a row. The informal style is the best choice for plants such as roses and cotoneaster that produce showy flowers or fruit, because you aren't constantly cutting off the flower buds, and for shrubs with an attractive growth habit, such as forsythia. Rather than making a plain green backdrop, an informal hedge is more likely to be a feature in its own right. Plan on an informal hedge if you are planting on the property line and don't have easy access to the other side for maintenance. Choose naturally small or columnar plants; rambling loose hedges may take up too much space in a small garden.

SHAPING A HEDGE

For formal and semiformal hedges, space the plants close together—generally 1 to 3 feet apart, depending on their natural spread and how quickly you want the hedge to fill in (as close as 6 inches for the smallest dwarf hedges). After planting, cut back the plants to ensure the hedge grows thickly at the base. Cut back large deciduous plants by about a third, and smaller ones to within several inches of the ground. Cut back fast-growing broad-leafed evergreen plants less severely. Slow-growing broad-leafed evergreens and conifers need a different treatment: shorten their lateral branches, but don't cut back the leaders.

During the first growing season, don't prune formal or semiformal hedges except to shorten any overly vigorous shoots. Each year thereafter until the hedge is filled in, cut back new growth by about half to encourage dense branching.

To develop the shape of a formal or semiformal hedge, you may need to use a wooden frame or a string stretched between stakes as a guide when you prune. Whatever shape you choose, be sure to slope the sides so that the bottom is wider than the top (see illustration at top of page 66). This will allow sunlight to reach the bottom of the hedge and stimulate growth there. If the

AERIAL CAMELLIA HEDGE

Designers Shari and Richard Sullivan pruned up a thicket of camellias in this narrow space along the side of their house to form a leafy screen over the boundary fence (it was their young son's idea to paint the trunks blue). See page 91 for information on "limbing up" an overgrown shrub to shape it like a tree. Alternatively, grow new plants and train them as standards; see page 75.

USING A WOODEN FRAME

A simple, inexpensive wooden frame consisting of 1 by 2s nailed together serves as a guide for shearing a formal hedge or selectively pruning a semiformal hedge.

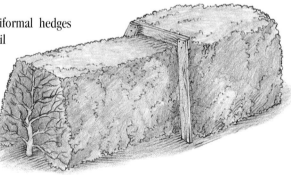

SLOPING THE SIDES OF A HEDGE

lower branches are shaded, they will grow more slowly and eventually die. Tapering the sides of very low hedges isn't necessary because they don't get tall enough to block sunlight.

An informal hedge needs the least shaping. Place the plants slightly closer together than their mature width (for example, 4 feet apart for plants that will spread 6 feet wide). During the first year, pinch off the branch tips to get full, bushy growth and to prevent holes from developing in the hedge. In the second year, if branches didn't form low enough, pinch again.

PRUNING AND TRIMMING MATURE HEDGES

For mature formal and semiformal hedges, shear or selectively cut back the new growth close to its point of origin, but don't remove it entirely. Do this pruning after the spring growth flush has stopped, to prevent the hedge from growing too big. Some formal hedges need only one shearing a year, but others will send forth new growth after the first trimming and will need to be pruned again. In mild-winter regions, you may find yourself pruning vigorous growers well into fall. In cold-winter areas, stop pruning at least a month before the first expected fall frost.

You can probably prune many semiformal hedges just once a year, in spring, with a few additional snips here and there during the growing season to keep the hedges neat. Trim conifer hedges regularly to avoid the necessity of a drastic cut that might reveal the hedge's bare interior; conifers generally won't resprout from old wood.

Prune informal hedges as you would prune the individual plants, as required for the species or variety you are growing. But try to keep the hedge looking uniform by thinning out branches on any overlarge plants and heading back the growth on smaller ones to encourage branching.

CHOOSING A VINE

Vines take up less ground space than hedges and can grow taller. Some vines are ideal for small, delicate screens, whereas others know no bounds. A few monster vines, such as ivy, will cover a college building if left unchecked and may push up the roof shingles and work their way inside. It's not necessarily a bad idea to choose a fast- and rampant-growing vine, but it will need regular, heavy pruning in a small space.

For aesthetic reasons, it's best to choose a vine with a scale that is naturally suited to the space. For a picket fence or thin wood or wire trellises, choose a relatively small, lightweight plant, such as a small clematis variety. Large, heavy vines—like passion vine *(Passiflora),* trumpet creeper *(Campsis),* and wisteria—need the sturdy support of a tall chain-link fence, a wall, or a roomy arbor with posts anchored in concrete.

Also consider your privacy needs: an evergreen vine on a trellis will provide privacy year-round, but it may be better to plant a deciduous vine, such as a grape, so that more sunlight can penetrate during the winter. Most deciduous vines have colorful foliage in the fall, and the tracery of bare stems, especially on a wall or plain fence, can be lovely in winter.

TYPES OF VINES

Vines are usually categorized by their climbing method: either they twine around supports naturally; they grasp on with tendrils, suction disks, or aerial rootlets; or they need tying.

Twining vines twist and spiral as they grow, coiling around a slender support, themselves, or nearby plants. Most twining vines can't encircle a large post without some help (see "Support for Vines" on the facing page). Wisteria, honeysuckle *(Lonicera),* jasmine, silver lace vine *(Polygonum aubertii),* and Carolina jessamine *(Gelsemium sempervirens)* are all twining vines.

CLIMBING METHODS

Twining stems

Tendrils

The tendrils on vines such as passion vine and clematis reach out and wrap around whatever is handy—a wire or cord, another stem of the vine, or an adjoining plant. Tendrils grow out straight until they make contact, then reflexively contract into a spiral to grasp their host. Vines with tendrils are ideal covers for open latticework such as chain-link fences and lath trellises.

Clinging vines adhere tightly to surfaces by means of suction disks at the ends of the tendrils or aerial rootlets along their stems. Boston ivy *(Parthenocissus)* and trumpet vine *(Distictis)* have suction disks at the end of tendrils; ivy *(Hedera)* and climbing hydrangea have rootlets. Be careful about where you plant clinging vines. They can get under and lift wood siding; they can also weaken the mortared joints between bricks and concrete blocks. Don't grow clinging vines on any surface you intend to paint or stain in the future because removing them is no easy task; the disks and rootlets will stubbornly stick to the surface, often out of your reach.

Vines with no means of attaching themselves, such as bougainvillea, will sprawl along the ground unless tied to a vertical support. Any kind of support will do, even a smooth wall if you can attach hardware to it to anchor the ties (see page 78). For other supports and suggested tying materials, see the section below.

SUPPORT FOR VINES

Trellises and latticework fences, which have large openings, suit nearly all vines; you simply weave the stems through the spaces. Most vines, however, will need help ascending the wide posts of sturdy arbors. You can give the vines something to grasp by stringing galvanized wires or cord through eyescrews or eye bolts inserted into the posts, or you can spiral the vines around the posts by hand and tie them in place. The type of tie you need depends on the vine. Good choices for lightweight plants include soft twine, raffia, wide rubber bands, and green plastic garden tape. For heavy vines, use rope or strips of canvas or rubber. Tie the ties loosely so as not to restrict growth.

Vines with no means of attaching will need securing at various points along their length, so you may have to use a ladder to affix ties if you want the vine to grow tall. A few of these vines—notably climbing roses and most types of bougainvillea—can hook themselves onto adjacent shrubs or trees with their thorns.

If you provide a support that allows a vine to climb by itself (a tree trunk for a clinging vine, for example), be prepared for the possibility that it will grow out of reach.

ARCHING ROSES

Left to their own devices, most climbing roses will produce a screen of vigorous long canes but make a paltry show of flowers. For more blooms, bend the canes into arches, which will redirect the plant's energy into forming growth buds along the canes. Most of these buds develop into flowering laterals, shoots about 8 to 16 inches long that produce flowers. A few of the more vigorous nonflowering shoots (growth laterals) will produce flowers if you arch them over, too.

Some shorter, stiff-caned climbers (pillar roses) will grow upright yet still produce flowering laterals, so they needn't be arched over. These more closely resemble floppy shrubs than climbers. Keep them erect by tying them to a pillar or other support.

Suction disks

Aerial rootlets

Needs tying

Wooden screens

A simple wooden screen has myriad uses in a small garden. It can hide a compost heap or give you some privacy from a neighbor's yard. The first screen described here is a permanent installation. The other two are portable; you can move the barrel screen to follow the movement of the sun during lunch, and the freestanding screen to make an alcove in different parts of the garden in different seasons.

A TREE POLE

A single "tree" pole covered with a vine might be all you need to obscure or take your eye away from something unsightly next door. A series of tree poles with swags of climbing roses along connecting ropes or wires, and perhaps a low hedge planted below, would make a magnificent architectural border for a terrace or lawn.

Buy either pressure-treated lumber or naturally decay-resistant materials, such as redwood or cedar heartwood. Construct the "trunk" of the pole with a pair of 2 by 4s any height you want. Position 1-by-4 spacers at equal intervals between the 2 by 4s, and create the "branches" at the top with 1 by 4s that are 18 inches long. Make contour cuts in the ends of the branches; if you want to get fancy, round or chamfer the trunk pieces with a router. Sink the trunk into a concrete footing as you would a fence post (see page 70).

A BARREL SCREEN

This portable planter can provide a little privacy and screen an undesirable view or the too-bright rays of the setting sun. Move it from place to place as you would an umbrella.

Buy an oak half-barrel at a nursery or garden supply store or use any large, sturdy wooden container at least 2 feet in diameter. Tack the metal barrel rings in place with roofing nails to keep them from slipping if the barrel dries out and shrinks. Turn the barrel over and bolt three casters in a triangle on the bottom. While the barrel is turned over, drill several $3/4$- to 1-inch-diameter holes in the bottom for drainage. To prevent weathering on the outside, brush on several coats of linseed oil. Let the coatings dry between applications. If you like, screw drawer pulls to opposite sides of the barrel to make it easier to move.

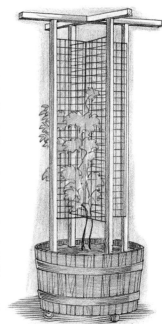

Next, build the trellis. For the uprights, cut surfaced (planed smooth) 2 by 2s into four $6\frac{1}{2}$-foot lengths; coat the lower $1\frac{1}{2}$ feet of each post with wood preservative. For the cross-support, cut an 8-foot 2 by 2 in half, then cut notches in the centers of the two pieces to form a lap joint. To make each notch, set the blade of a portable circular saw at half the thickness of the wood; make two cuts to outline

CUTTING NOTCHES

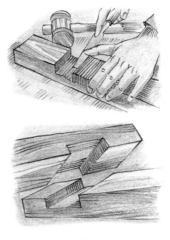

the joint's shoulder, then make several more cuts in the "waste area" inside the lines. Use a chisel to remove the waste wood and to smooth the bottom of the joint, then fit the pieces together, as shown at left.

Screw the cross-support to the tops of the four uprights with $2\frac{1}{2}$-inch screws. The distance between outside edges of two opposing posts should equal the inside diameter of the barrel bottom.

Slip the trellis inside the barrel, spread the legs against the sides, and screw L-brackets to the legs and the barrel bottom.

Cut a 4-foot-square piece of plastic-coated welded wire mesh in half and snip off the sharp ends. Bend one piece lengthwise to fit between two adjacent posts about 5 inches down from the top. Position the cut edges of the mesh about $1/2$ inch in from edges of the posts and staple the mesh in place every 6 inches. Install the second screen on the opposite side. If it doesn't quite fit because it bumps the first screen, offset it slightly.

Fill the barrel with soil and plant a vine to cover each mesh panel. Annual vines may need support from netting or string until they reach the wire mesh.

A FREESTANDING SCREEN

Building a basic lath screen with crisscrossing uprights and crosspieces is quite easy. The screen shown here is composed of two lath grids in simple frames joined with hinges. The posts are sunk in sand to make the screen portable.

Choose naturally decay-resistant woods, such as redwood or cedar heartwood. Use 1 by 2s for the lath pieces: for each lath grid, you'll need six uprights 5 feet tall and nine crosspieces 3½ feet wide. Buy 2 by 4s for the frame posts and the tops of the frames: for each frame, you'll need two 7½-foot-long posts and a 3½-foot-long crosspiece. Build the lath grid before sizing the frame.

Join the finished frames with three bifold hinges. To sink the posts in sand, dig three 2-foot-deep holes (the center hole needs to be wider), pour 4 inches of sand in the bottoms of the holes, position the posts, then fill the holes with more sand, packing it in firmly.

SPACE DIVIDER

A panel of lattice suspended in a sturdy frame at the back of a raised bed separates a dining area from other areas of the garden—and the neighbors. A latticework divider is far superior to a solid screen in a small garden because it provides a sense of privacy while also allowing a breeze and sunlight to stream through.

MAKING A FREESTANDING SCREEN

1 Lay the lath uprights face down on a flat surface, then lay out the crosspieces. Space the pieces equidistantly, on approximately 8-inch centers, to make the grid. Place a dab of waterproof glue where the pieces cross. Then nail or screw each intersection. When the finished grid is flipped back over, the fasteners will be out of sight.

2 Size the frame pieces to fit around the finished grid, with the sides of the frame flanking the top piece. Join the sides to the top using glue and countersunk screws.

3 Slide the lath grid inside the frame. Drive in screws from the sides of the frame to keep the grid in place.

FENCES

Low, open fences are mere markers of boundaries. They are polite reminders that the front lawn is private property, but they don't obstruct the view into or out of the garden; they are friendly fences. Other fences need to be tall and solid for security reasons. In between are hundreds of designs that aim to provide some privacy or sense of enclosure without looming darkly over a small garden or blocking a pleasant breeze.

HOW TALL? HOW SOLID?

In each part of your garden, consider exactly how much privacy you need and keep the screening as low and open as possible so that you don't create unnecessary areas of deep shade or an unpleasant boxed-in effect. If you want privacy while sitting on the patio, perhaps the fence need only be chest high; if you want to block an unpleasant view, perhaps an attractive open trellis would suffice to distract the eye. You can make an open fence more solid in places where you need privacy by planting shrubs or rambling roses there. Don't build a solid fence for shelter from wind. A fence with gaps between the siding filters the wind into a breeze, whereas a solid fence simply tips the wind right over the fence.

BOARD FENCES

Digging the postholes is the hardest part of building a board fence. For fences 3 to 6 feet tall, the posts need to be set at least 2 feet deep (3 feet deep for the end posts). For taller fences, the rule of thumb is one-third the post length. Use a pick and shovel to dig the holes or find a local tool rental company and look for a posthole (clamshell) digger or a power auger; in deep, loose soils, a hand-operated auger may work well.

Board fences are composed of three elements: posts, rails, and siding. The posts, often 4 by 4s, are set in concrete, usually at intervals of 6 to 8 feet. Two rails, 2 by 4s, run between the posts, one at the top of the posts and one 6 to 8 inches above the ground. The siding, usually about 1 inch thick, is attached to the rails.

Board fences are readily available in panel form if you don't want to build from scratch. The panels are usually 6 feet wide, and they come in various heights; some board designs have an open lattice top, which makes a lighter-looking fence. Suppliers sell the posts and rails along with the panels; they fit together with nails or brackets. For all lumber fences, choose pressure-treated lumber or naturally decay-resistant redwood or cedar heartwood. For a fence close to the house, choose smooth, finished wood.

BUILDING A BOARD FENCE

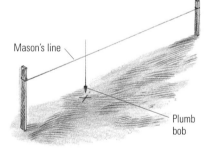

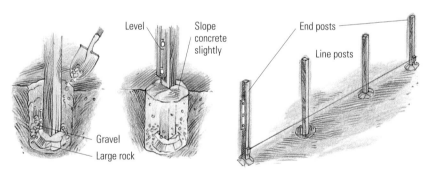

1 First, mark each end or corner post location with a stake. Run mason's line between the stakes, as shown. With chalk, mark the remaining post locations on the line. Using a level or plumb bob, transfer each mark to the ground and drive in additional stakes. Then dig holes 6 inches deeper than the post depth and two and a half to three times the post's diameter.

2 Place a rock at the base of each hole and add 4 to 6 inches of gravel. Starting with an end or corner post, set the post in the hole and shovel in concrete, tamping it down with a broomstick or capped steel pipe. Adjust the post for plumb with a level. Continue filling until the concrete extends 1 to 2 inches above ground level, then slope it away from the post to divert water.

3 Repeat for the other end or corner post, making sure the faces of the posts are parallel and plumb. (After setting posts in fresh concrete, you have about 20 minutes to align them before the concrete hardens.) To align the line posts, tack 1-by-2 spacer blocks to the end posts, string mason's line between them, and set each post a block's thickness from the line, filling and leveling the concrete as described in step 2. Let cure for 2 days. Remove the blocks.

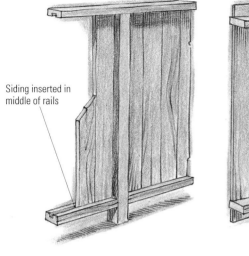

Siding inserted in middle of rails

Siding installed in alternating panels

CODES AND ETIQUETTE

Before you set the first post, check your local building and zoning laws. Local ordinances often specify the minimum setback from the street for a front fence and a maximum height for front, side, and back fences. In some communities, it is mandatory to erect a board fence so that the best side (the side to which the siding is nailed) is what the neighbors see; you get the side with the framing. In other communities, the choice is left up to you. Good-neighbor fences (above) look the same on both sides.

AIRY TRELLIS PANELS

A trellis on the fence top and alternating panels of trellis in the fence itself make this an airy, friendly-looking boundary between a side garden and the street. It's best to design the trellis as part of the fence, as was done so beautifully here, but a trellis can be mounted to the top of an existing board fence to give a garden more privacy. Extend each fence post with an extra length of post, joining the two with a metal post anchor or two long 2 by 2s nailed over the join on opposite sides of the fence. Attach the trellis to the posts and grow vines up them to cover the joins.

Butted joint   Notched joint   Lapping joint

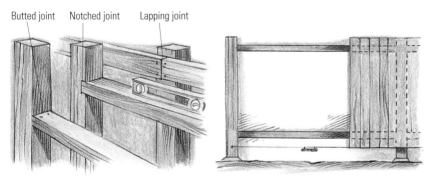

4 Brush on wood preservative where the rails and posts will meet. Then fasten one end of each rail; check the level with a helper and secure the other end. You can butt rails against the post and toenail them, notch them in (cut notches before installing posts), or lap them over the sides or top of each post. If you're planning to use lapping joints, the fence will be stronger if you use rails that span at least three posts.

5 Cut siding boards to the same length. Stretch and level a line from post to post to mark the bottom of the siding. Check the first board for plumb, then secure it to the rails with galvanized nails that are three times as long as the board's thickness. Add additional boards, checking alignment as you go. Redwood can be left to weather naturally, but fir or pine should be painted or stained.

SLOPES AND LEVELS

To a designer's eye, a slope in a garden is a blessing. It's an opportunity to introduce steps and walls, which not only provide visual interest and drama, but also break up a single space into two or more spaces, making the garden seem larger. The construction need not be technically difficult; rustic steps and a low retaining wall are feasible projects even for a beginner.

DEGREES OF SLOPE

Most gardeners want to have a level space close to the house so they can sit outdoors on balmy days and flat land on which to garden comfortably. But it's not necessary to terrace every part of a slope with retaining walls and steps. Banks and sloping paths that maintain the garden's natural contours are attractive garden features, too.

Several design options are available for shallow and medium slopes, fewer for very steep slopes. The simplest and least expensive way to create level space on a steep lot is to build a deck. Tall trees planted on the slope around it bring foliage to the deck height, lessening the feeling of being perched above ground level.

A STEPPING-STONE STAIRCASE

A stepping-stone staircase is a relatively easy and inexpensive way to take a path up a slope. It works particularly well in an informal area of the garden and where foot traffic isn't high. Choose extralarge stones, at least 20 inches deep, 2 feet wide, and 6 to 8 inches thick.

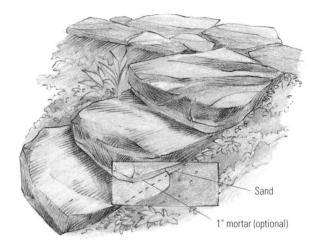

Sand

1" mortar (optional)

Starting at the downhill end of the slope, excavate a hole for the first stone. Make it as deep as the stone is thick, measuring on the uphill side. Spread 2 inches of sand in the bottom of the hole, wet the sand, and tamp it with a hand tamper. (If your soil is unstable or drains poorly, dig a much deeper hole and install 4 to 6 inches of tamped gravel before adding the sand.) Lay the

SHALLOW SLOPE

To create a level front lawn, the grade has been raised at the street behind a retaining wall. Another retaining wall in front of the house allows for a level path to the side yard. In the back, steps lead up to terraces that create level areas for a lawn, a play area, and planting beds.

MEDIUM SLOPE

Low retaining walls create four different levels in front. Steps, a retaining wall, and low banks solve the slope problem in the backyard. The lawn is a gentle slope, so that the mower need not be lifted or pulled up and down steps.

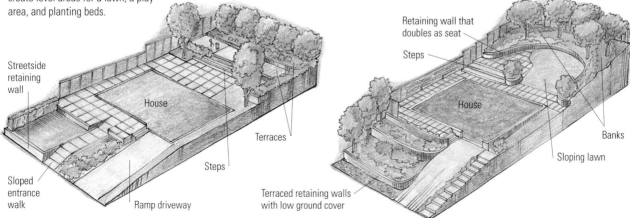

Streetside retaining wall

House

Terraces

Steps

Sloped entrance walk

Ramp driveway

Retaining wall that doubles as seat

Steps

House

Banks

Sloping lawn

Terraced retaining walls with low ground cover

stone in the hole and twist it into the sand until it is level and firmly embedded. The surface of the stone should sit about 2 inches above grade so that soil doesn't wash onto it after a rain.

When the first stone is securely embedded, position the next stone. In gentle sections of the path, space the stones as you would for a stepping-stone path, leaving gaps of 4 to 6 inches between them. Where the slope is steep, overlap the stones a few inches for stability. You can also spread a 1-inch layer of mortar on the back of the lower step to bond them where they touch.

A SIMPLE MODULAR RETAINING WALL

A retaining wall holds back soil, allowing you to create level terraces behind and in front of it. It's also useful for drawing attention to a change in grade, as a design detail. A low, fairly stable slope can be retained by one of the simple modular masonry systems developed for the do-it-yourselfer. These systems consist of interlocking concrete blocks with rough finishes like split rock. A planter version is available, with a hollow center for soil and plants.

A modular block wall needs a simple gravel footing and gravel backfill with a drainpipe—no concrete work or mortar. The blocks interlock in such a way that they create a uniform setback into the slope, so you don't need to batter (tilt the face of) the wall. Choose a dark-colored block so that it will blend more easily into the garden foliage, and break up the angular lines by planting trailing plants on top of the wall and tall, bushy plants at the base.

To prepare a foundation for a modular system, dig a trench 2 feet wide and 6 inches deeper than the thickness of the block. String mason's twine to mark the front edge of the wall. Pour 6 inches of gravel into the trench and compact it firmly with a hand tamper. Check that the base is level.

Lay the first row of blocks on the gravel footing against the front edge of the trench. If the blocks have a rear lip, install this first row upside down and backward, so that the block surface resting on the gravel is flat and the lip is facing up at the front of the wall. Check that the blocks are level and aligned with the mason's twine.

Lay perforated drainpipe, perforated side down, on the gravel behind the wall, with the open end extending toward the storm sewer or a suitable surface drainage area. Pack gravel under the capped end of the pipe as needed to ensure that the open end slopes downhill.

Lay the second row of blocks, staggering the vertical joints in a running bond pattern. To make the ends of the wall flush, use half blocks, if they are available, or cut a block in half with a masonry saw. Backfill the space behind the wall with gravel, and tamp the gravel firmly with a hand tamper. Place the subsequent rows of blocks in the same manner, backfilling and compacting the gravel after laying each row.

Lay landscape fabric over the gravel backfill before you replace the topsoil and plant behind the wall. The fabric will help prevent soil from clogging the backfilled area.

PICNICKING STEPS

This slope is gentle enough that the steps here might not have been necessary from a purely practical standpoint, but the horizontal lines of the risers swing beautifully up the slope, inviting you into the garden. Note the gracious dimensions of the stairs: small risers, the thickness of the stone, and treads large enough to picnic on. To save on stone costs, you might make the landings of gravel, but if the steps are widely spaced, be sure they are extra-large and visible or people may not notice one and trip.

Design: Conni Cross

A MODULAR RETAINING WALL

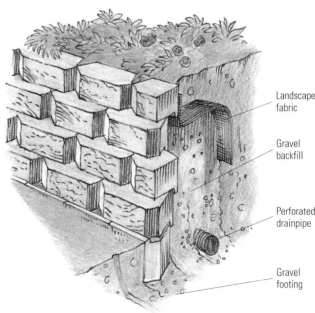

Landscape fabric

Gravel backfill

Perforated drainpipe

Gravel footing

TOWERING PLANTS, TRELLISES, ARCHES

Trees, vine supports, and other tall garden elements add a third dimension of space that is especially valuable in a small yard. The vertical lines lift the eye up, away from the small garden floor, and if you grow some plants up off the ground, you can plant more plants under them, which will make the garden more lush.

OPTIONS FOR CREATING HEIGHT

Trees expand the garden dramatically; their tops reach far over our heads and touch the sky. To avoid creating too much shade in a small space, choose tall, skinny trees or select a small tree with delicate branching, such as a Japanese maple, that lets light filter through the leaves to the garden floor. Plant a diminutive ground cover or pave the area beneath the tree, and the tree will seem even taller.

You can also introduce a few vertical plants in a shrub or perennial border to direct the eye upward. Look for plants shaped like exclamation points or towering masses with airy, branching stems. Good choices include foxgloves, delphiniums, crambe, hollyhocks, and ornamental grasses with graceful seed heads. For more suggestions for towering flowering plants, see page 110.

Think tall as you shop for pots and ornaments. Collect tall urns, obelisks, pyramid-shaped wire topiary frames, trellises and poles for vines, simple arches, and plinths and pedestals to raise pots to eye level. You can also create height by stacking your unused pots in tall columns and storing prunings and firewood in tall piles. In the vegetable garden, you might build a tepee for pole beans to climb, using four 8-foot-long pieces of bamboo lashed together at the top.

Vertical plants

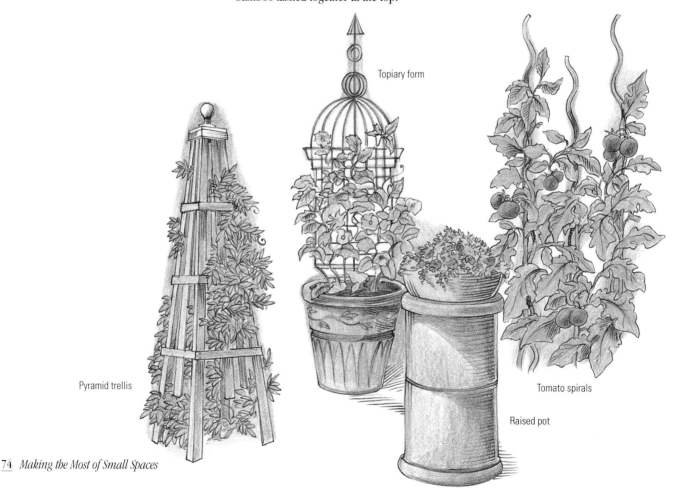

Topiary form

Pyramid trellis

Raised pot

Tomato spirals

TRAINING SHRUBS INTO STANDARDS

Because standards put foliage and flowers up high, they're also useful for drawing the eye off a small garden floor. You can buy shrubs that have already been trained as standards (they look like lollipops with a spindly stem taped to a stake) or you can train your own. To make a standard look more elegant, grow it in a square of clipped boxwood or yew.

For small standards (2 to 4 feet high), try fuchsia, lantana, rosemary, ivy *(Hedera)*, or a Southern Indica hybrid azalea; for larger standards (4 to 6 feet), consider camellia, hibiscus, holly, lilac, pyracantha, wisteria, some flowering viburnums *(V. japonicum, V. odoratissimum, V. tinus* 'Robustum'), or witch hazel. If you want a standard rose, also called a tree rose, you can grow your own with a cutting from a large climber or shrub rose, but it's easiest to buy one already trained. (Rose standards are usually created by grafting together three rose plants: a rootstock; an interstock to form a strong, straight trunk; and the flowering top variety.)

To train a shrub into a standard, begin with a young specimen of your chosen plant. At planting time, remove all stems except the strongest one, which will form the trunk, and tie the stem to a stake. Keep the lateral shoots on it for the first year to nourish the trunk but shorten them so they won't compete with the leader. Let the stem grow until it reaches the point where you want the foliage to branch out; cut back any further stem growth and allow buds just below the stem cut to develop into shoots. Pinch off the shoot tips to stimulate more branching until a treelike top is formed. To keep the standard in good shape, frequently pinch off the shoot tips in the crown and remove any growth along the trunk. You may have to stake the plant permanently if it's too weak to stay upright on its own.

Trained standard

SHOPPING FOR A TRELLIS

A trellis can be a freestanding piece of garden architecture or merely a plant support that's mounted on a fence. In either case, since most vines aren't at their best in winter, it's worth buying a trellis that's at least a little interesting to look at bare.

Choose a trellis material and level of detailing that match the character of the garden. Twig and branch trellises are particularly suitable for a cottage garden or vegetable beds; some metal trellises are copies of antiques and look best in the most elegant spaces. Trellises made of wood can be plain and casual or topped with finials so they look architectural.

Consider the effects of the weather on the trellis material. Will it age beautifully? Redwood and cedar turn a pleasing natural gray; uncoated copper weathers to a handsome verdigris. On the other hand, some metal trellises will rust if left outdoors all year, and some wooden ones will rot. Ask the supplier how long the material will last. If it will rot when in contact with damp soil, consider mounting it on rot-resistant supports (see "Installing a Trellis" on page 76).

A short trellis is adequate to support a low-growing vine, such as black-eyed Susan vine or a small clematis; taller vines, such as bower vine *(Pandorea jasminoides)*, need taller supports. For a rampant grower like silver lace vine or wisteria, you'll need a large, extrasturdy trellis—the kind that has to be sunk into concrete if it's freestanding or attached with lag bolts to a wall. A vine should also suit the style of the trellis. Choose a delicate vine for a topiary trellis and train and prune it so that the trellis's elegant outline always shows.

Metal trellis

Woven wood trellis

Continued >

INSTALLING A TRELLIS

To install a trellis in the ground, just push the feet into the soil beside a wall or in a planter box, plant a vine, and wrap the stems around the supports (using plant ties when needed). For a wood trellis that may rot in contact with damp soil, consider driving a pressure-treated wood stake, a length of steel reinforcing bar, or a galvanized pipe sleeve into the ground and fastening the trellis to it using screws, bolts, or wires. If the trellis has posts, you can anchor them in a concrete footing (see page 70).

Use rust-resistant screws, nails, or—for heavy structures—lag screws to attach a trellis to a wooden fence or to wood house siding (be careful not to plant vigorous clinging vines that may creep under the siding; see page 67). Make wood spacer blocks to create at least 4 inches of space between the trellis and the supporting structure for good air circulation. If your trellis is heavy, attach it to wall framing or posts, not just to thin siding or fence boards.

You can attach a light trellis to a masonry wall with concrete screws. For a heavier trellis, drill holes into the masonry, insert expanding anchors, and thread a galvanized screw or lag screw into each anchor.

MAKING A BAMBOO TRELLIS

The bamboo poles available in lengths of 4 to 12 feet from many nurseries and mail-order sources are a surprisingly strong and durable material for a trellis and, of course, much lighter in weight than lumber. For a large trellis, choose 1½-inch bamboo poles; for a small one, you might use ¾-inch poles. Avoid using the "split" bamboo for support pieces; it's not as durable. (To make a simple trellis using wood, see the instructions for the freestanding screen on page 69.)

To make the bamboo trellis shown below, lay out the horizontal crosspieces at even intervals on a flat surface. Then place the vertical poles so they alternate in front of and behind the crosspieces. Bind the poles where they cross, using either 15-gauge copper wire or precut pieces of galvanized wire (available from bamboo suppliers). Feed the

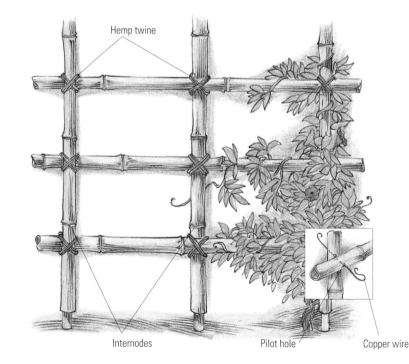

Hemp twine

Internodes Pilot hole Copper wire

VIEWS OF THE SKY

A mobile of gazing balls, sparkling with light, takes the eye up through the trees to the sky. It's worth searching for ways to lift the eye off the garden floor and out into the wider landscape, even if it's an urban one. People like to see out, and a view of the sky or a slice of the city or your neighbor's spring-flowering tree increases the feeling of space in a small yard. Ornaments on a rooftop, such as a weather vane or a decorative molding on the eaves of a garden shed, also draw the eye toward the sky.

Design: Simple

wire through oversize pilot holes drilled all the way through both pieces, as shown on facing page, then twist the ends together at the back with a pair of sturdy pliers. Be sure to wear gloves to protect your hands. For a traditional Japanese look, cover the wire with decorative hemp. To make the trellis less open, weave split bamboo or slim bundles of bamboo branches between the poles.

Because bamboo poles will rot when the ends are buried, slip the trellis poles over pipes set in the soil (the bamboo's solid internodes will keep the poles from sliding down the pipes) or suspend the trellis between cedar, redwood, or pressure-treated posts. Cut the tops of the poles just above an internode, so rain won't collect in them.

MAKING AN ARCH

An arch is often used in a small garden to frame a view along a path or to mark the threshold between one area and another. Many prefabricated arches are available, ranging from simple metal hoops to ornately finished lumber arches that are big enough to sit inside.

For the do-it-yourselfer, the simplest arch consists of three trellises—two to form the sides and one for a roof—and diagonal braces at the top. The roof should be at least 6 feet 8 inches high (the height of an interior door) and, if the arch will straddle a pathway, the opening should be at least 1 foot wider than the path. You could use almost any material—lath, bamboo, plumbing pipe, reinforcing bar, or the rustic saplings shown here. Consider building several arches, lining them up, and tying them together with crosspieces to form a tunnel or rustic pergola.

To make this arch, first build three ladder trellises using saplings at least 1½ inches thick. Nail the saplings together from the back. (Drill pilot holes to use as guides so the crooked, slippery pieces won't jump around while you nail; if necessary, clamp or tape them together while you work.) Then, for added stability, wrap the saplings together with wire or twine.

You'll need to add diagonal braces at the top corners to lock the arch together. (If you want an arch with a rounded top, make just the two side ladders, using long, pliable saplings, such as willow cut within the past 24 hours. Set the two ladders in the ground to form the sides of the arch, bend the tops toward each other until they overlap by several inches, and wire them together quickly.) Once the basic structure is intact, nail on decorative twigs or woven vines to your heart's content.

To help prevent the wood from rotting in the soil, wire the arch to pipes set in the soil; attach it to cedar, redwood, or pressure-treated posts driven into the ground; or set the uprights inside galvanized pipe sleeves.

ARCH TURNED BOWER

Place an arch against a hedge or wall, cover the frame with vining plants, move a bench inside, and the arch is no longer a portal to pass through but a garden retreat. Dress it up by placing pots on either side and giving it a separate floor. To please the senses, plant fragrant plants—perhaps ones that bloom at twilight—and keep the rest of the world at bay with the sweet sounds of a fountain.

ESPALIERS

Many shrubs, trees, and vines can be made to fit into a small space by training their branches against a wall or fence. Plants can be espaliered rather loosely, or painstakingly pruned into dramatic straight lines. Whichever style suits you, get a pair of narrow-nosed pruning shears so you don't scrape your knuckles working in tight spaces, and save yourself some work by applying very little growth-promoting nitrogen fertilizer to the plants.

CHOOSING ESPALIER PLANTS

For formal geometric espaliers, choose plants that have pliant young branches so they are easy to train; for informal fan shapes, choose plants with a naturally arching form (a list of plants that are easy to espalier appears on page 107). If you are planning to plant against a south-facing wall in a warm climate, choose a heat-tolerant plant or consider an alternative wall with a cooler exposure; if the wall is light in color, you may need to wrap or whitewash an exposed trunk to prevent sunburn, and you should keep a dense cover of leaves on the plant to protect the branches.

Plants have different flowering (and fruiting) habits; some flower only on the current season's growth, others on only the previous season's growth, and still others on both new and old growth. Because you'll be pruning new growth heavily for the most rigid geometric espalier patterns, check a plant's flowering habit before you buy if you want lots of flowers (or fruit).

TYPES OF SUPPORT

All but the most informal espaliers (see "Flat and Informal" on the facing page) are trained by tying branches to a trellis or wires. If the espalier is to go against a wall, you can build a sturdy trellis and set it in the ground 8 to 12 inches away from the wall so there will be adequate air circulation around the plant. Or, you can screw eye bolts into the wall and thread 14-gauge galvanized wires between them (see illustration at right); put the lowest wire 18 inches off the ground and those above it 18 to 24 inches apart, leaving as much space as you can between the wires and the wall for air circulation. For a freestanding espalier fence (shown below), use the same spacing between wires.

Wires can be attached directly to stone, concrete, or brick walls (above). Drill holes for 5- to 7-inch eye bolts 4 feet apart, insert expansion shields (preferably lead) into the holes, and screw the eye bolts into the shields. String the wire through the eye bolts and twist to secure.

To create a simple freestanding espalier fence (left), stretch wires between 4-by-4 posts sunk well in the ground. Incorporate turnbuckles at both ends of each wire to tighten as the espaliered plant matures.

ESPALIERING A FRUIT TREE

Of all the fruit trees, apples and pears are the most obliging about having their branches manipulated into precise geometric patterns, such as the horizontal cordon shown on the facing page. They have pliant branches, and their fruiting spurs (short shoots that form flowers and bear fruit) are long lived, so they continue fruiting even on the oldest wood.

For a large wall or fence, buy a tree on a semidwarf rootstock; for a smaller area, choose one on a dwarf rootstock. You can start out with an unbranched whip or a tree that has a few branches. If the variety needs cross-pollination, plant at least one compatible tree close by in the garden or espalier the trees together. Avoid choosing tip-bearing apple varieties, such as 'Granny Smith', 'Jonathan', and 'Rome Beauty'; as well as trees on standard stocks.

Plant your tree during its winter dormancy. Choose a location that receives full sun; in hot-summer areas, however, avoid planting against a light-colored south-facing wall or you'll cook your fruit. Position the tree 6 to 8 inches away from the wall or fence to allow room for the trunk to grow. For a row of espaliered fruit trees, set trees at least 6 feet apart.

The espaliering process begins at planting. If you are starting with a whip, head it back at or just above the lowest support wire, retaining two buds facing in opposite directions and a third bud to grow vertically. If you are starting with a branched tree, see the first illustration below. During the training process, use plastic nursery ties, raffia, bits of string, or clear grafting or budding tape for tying the branches to the wires. To prevent one branch of a pair from outstripping the other in growth, you can adjust the branch angles—raising a branch to increase growth, lowering a branch to reduce it.

CREATING A HORIZONTAL CORDON

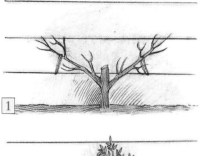

1 At planting, select two branches for the first tier; remove all other shoots and head back the leader to a bud just above the bottom wire. Bend branches at a 45-degree angle and secure them to the wire.

2 In the first growing season, gradually tighten the branch ties until the branches are horizontal by season's end. Hold the newly sprouted leader so it's erect and tie it to the second-tier wire.

3 In the first dormant season, head back the leader close to the second wire. Select two branches for a second tier and remove competing shoots. Prune the lateral growth on the first-tier branches back to three buds.

4 In the second growing season, gradually bring the second-tier branches to a horizontal position. Keep the leader upright and tie it to the third-tier wire.

5 Repeat the process for a fourth wire, if you have one. When the leader reaches the top wire, cut it back to just above the top branch. Keep horizontal branches from outgrowing the available space by pruning back the ends to downward-facing side branches in late spring and summer.

FLAT AND INFORMAL

An informal espalier—one without a precise pattern—is very easy to make. You just plant a tree or shrub in front of a structure such as a wall, trellis, or fence; allow it to branch naturally; and then remove any growth that juts out too far from the structure. What grows flat, stays, and what doesn't, you trim away (be diligent about the pruning, though; check the plant every few weeks during the growing season). Any plant that develops a horizontal branch pattern naturally, such as the cotoneaster shown here against a stucco wall, is a good candidate for an informal espalier.

CONTAINER GARDENS

Container gardening allows you to put plants in the soilless areas of the garden—along the garden paths, on the stairs, in the sitting areas, and even on the tops and sides of walls and fences. If decorating makes you nervous, remember that you can't go wrong with the simplest approach: one of the most satisfying and effective designs is a circle or line of identical plain containers all planted with the same kind of plant.

PUTTING POTS TO WORK

Pairs of pots have a natural place as markers on either side of a front entrance, a gate, a flight of steps, or the midpoint of a path. Think of them as sentinels, and give them lots of presence: for example, plant them with trees that have a strong outline or interesting branching structure or with any plant that has bold foliage or flowers; or use fancy large pots and set trellises inside them.

Medium and small containers look most effective in groups. You can make a strong focal point with them, perhaps to take the eye off a less attractive feature in the garden, or use them to dress up an entrance, a plain patio, or the top of a wall. You may be able to arrange many different plants artistically, generating a balance of forms that satisfies the eye. If you find that difficult, resort to a little geometry: place the pots in a line or in concentric circles with the largest and tallest at the center; arrange them roughly in tiers, with the largest pot at the back; or set them on tiered staging. To keep moisture from staining decks or patios and to prevent the decay of wood surfaces, elevate pots on wood blocks, cleats, or trivets.

CHOOSING CONTAINERS

Almost anything will make a fine plant pot—a galvanized metal trough, a classic wooden Versailles tub, an old terra-cotta pot, even a camping pan or bucket—as long as you can punch drainage holes in the base. Match the shape of the container to the habit of your plant: use a dish or shallow trough for a succulent, a dumpy pot for an ornamental cabbage, a tall pot for a tree. Alternatively, create an interesting contrast, for example, by setting a clipped plant ball or pyramid in a square tub.

PAINTING POTS

Unglazed clay pots and wooden containers (that have been sanded first) can be painted with latex paint. Apply a base coat of paint with a roller or paintbrush on the outside of the pot. Let it dry. Then apply a second coat or create patterns with several different colors of paint. Use masking tape to define geometric shapes; spatter paint onto the pot by flicking it off a brush; or stamp the pot with paint-coated squares, triangles, or circles cut from a sponge.

A color wash lends an aged patina to an ordinary unglazed clay or concrete pot. You'll need a cream-colored exterior latex paint for the base coat. For the wash, choose three colors of latex paint that complement one another, such as apricot, green, and umber; or use colors that match the plants that will go in the pot.

Start by covering the pot with the cream-colored base paint. Let the paint dry. In a plastic container, mix ¼ cup of the first wash color with ¼ cup of low-luster paint sealer (available from a paint store) and ½ cup of water. Starting at the top of the pot, brush the mix onto the pot, using a scrunched up piece of cheesecloth to blot the paint

drips and mottle the color (for the least uniform look, blot lightly in some areas, heavily in others). Let the first color dry. Make a second mix with the second color, apply it, blot, and let dry. For the third color, use just paint and water: pour some paint onto a plate, dip the paintbrush first into the paint and then into water, and brush the paint onto the pot. Blot to absorb drips (or let some remain) and to distribute the color. Let the pot dry completely before planting.

PLANTING CONTAINERS

Use a potting mix designed for containers. This kind of mix is lighter than garden soil and fast draining, and supplies ample nutrients for the plants. Some of the potting mixes include gels, or soil polymers, that absorb and retain water and dissolved nutrients, keeping them available near plant roots. The gels let you stretch the time between waterings, which is especially valuable in dry climates. If a potting mix doesn't contain gels, you can mix them in yourself in the manufacturer's recommended proportions.

Water plants in their nursery pots before transplanting them into containers. Ease out stubborn plants by running a knife around the inside edge of the pot or laying the pot on its side and rolling it from side to side gently. You may need to cut metal cans. Refrain from yanking on the stem or trunk of the plant or you'll damage the roots. Separate any matted and tangled roots so that they'll grow out into the new soil.

Pour enough potting mix into the container to hold the top of the plant root ball about 1 inch below the rim of the container. Moisten the mix, position the plant, fill in around it with more moist potting mix, and press the mix firmly to remove air pockets around the roots. Water the container. As a last step, check that the plant isn't planted too deep, which can cause rot; if necessary, lift the plant and pack more potting mix underneath it.

CARING FOR POTTED PLANTS

Watering is the most important aspect of caring for container plants. Potted plants dry out much quicker than plants in the ground. The problem is made worse if your containers are porous and they are in a hot, windy place. When the soil is drying out too quickly, consider mulching the soil surface with pebbles or bark, grouping pots close together so that they shade one another, switching to containers of less porous materials, or repotting into larger containers. A drip irrigation system with an automatic timer is helpful. When small pots have become dangerously dry, sink them into a tub of water so the water covers the pot rims but not the plants, and let them soak for half an hour.

Container plants generally need regular fertilizer throughout the growing season, starting 1 to 2 or 4 to 6 weeks after planting, depending on whether the potting mix had fertilizer in it. Liquid and controlled-release granular fertilizers are safer to use than dry fertilizer, which in a container may burn plant roots.

SINGLE AND UNPLANTED

A single pot can serve as a focal point or as a surprise. As a focal point, it needs to be extralarge, like the one shown here at the Little & Lewis sculpture garden on Bainbridge Island, Washington. You can make a large pot seem larger by raising it on a pedestal or a few bricks or by framing the view of it through an arch or an arching tree branch. You might also flank it with architectural plants or other containers to increase the drama.

To make the container work as a surprise, place it out of view of the main stopping places in the garden—perhaps tuck it back into a flower border, under a tree, or in a recess in a hedge—so that people come upon it suddenly as they pass by.

WATER FEATURES

Water is a lively, natural ornament for a garden of any size. A simple water bowl pulls a picture of the sky down into the garden. Add plants and fish to create an intriguing underwater world full of color, shadows, and movement; or add a fountain for soothing music that changes with the breeze and masks sounds of neighbors or nearby traffic.

CHOOSING AND PLACING WATER BOWLS

Any container that's watertight can make a simple reflection pool. For the best reflections, find a container with an extrawide opening at the top and a dark interior. Aluminum and glazed ceramic containers are interesting because they gleam when wet. Stone and unglazed bowls develop an interesting patina with age.

Experiment to find the best places for water bowls in your garden. Set up a bowl somewhere and check the reflection as you approach it along the path or look down on it from the deck. (If it's too cumbersome to keep filling and emptying the bowl as you move it around the garden, you can test the reflection by simply putting a mirror across the top of the bowl in different locations.) In an open area, a water-filled bowl will reflect the sky and sparkle in the sunlight. Under a tree, the water surface will capture the dark undersides of the leaves and pinpricks of light that flicker through the foliage. The reflections will change depending on the position of the sun in relation to the object and your eye.

If a small bowl is overshadowed by foliage or adjacent structures, raise the bowl on bricks or pavers or put it on top of a pedestal or wall to catch reflections of the sky. To display a container with an attractive outline, set it in an open area; if its shape is unattractive, consider nestling it among plants or sinking it into the ground like a tiny pond. Have at least one bowl that you can move easily as the seasons change: place it under daffodils in spring, move it into the roses later, then take it under a maple tree in fall to catch pictures of the changing leaf colors between the fallen leaves floating on the surface.

FLOATING WATER HYACINTH

Once the bowl is in its final position, use a carpenter's level to check that the rim is perfectly even before filling the bowl with water. If it isn't, adjust it by shimming up the container or moistening the soil underneath it and screwing the container into the ground until the rim is level. Then fill with water. When a bowl is full, even a slight tilt will be evident in the water line, and a large container will be too heavy and awkward to reposition.

To ornament the water a little, drop in a floating plant, such as water hyacinth *(Eichhornia crassipes)* or water lettuce *(Pistia stratiotes),* or place pebbles or tumbled colored glass in the bottom of the container. To clean the container periodically, empty the water and scrub the interior with a stiff brush.

MAKING A WATER LILY GARDEN

To plant a water lily, you'll need a container at least 2 feet across, with a capacity of at least 25 gallons. A wooden half-barrel is a popular choice. Be sure to buy a clean one (wine or old paint will leach into the water from the wood) and make it watertight by lining the inside with a sheet of black plastic pond liner or by keeping the staves wet to the top of the barrel (the staves will shrink if they dry out, and water will leak between them). To prevent water from evaporating through the sides, first coat the interior with asphalt emulsion or epoxy paint; the same advice holds true for unglazed clay containers. A metal trough from a feed-and-grain store holds about 170 gallons and has space enough for reeds and other marginal (shallow-water) plants, as well as a lily. If you choose a metal container, consider sinking it into the ground to help reduce fluctuations in the water temperature, which, if severe, can stress plants and fish.

There are two types of water lily: hardy and tropical. Hardy lilies are easier to grow because you can plant them anytime during the growing season—from early spring through October in mild climates—and leave them in the bottom of the water garden through the winter as long as all the water doesn't freeze. (If the water is likely to freeze, remove the rhizomes and store them wrapped in moist sand in a cool place indoors.) Tropicals are larger, more prolific bloomers (some bloom at night), but they are cold sensitive, so in all but the balmiest climates most gardeners treat them as annuals and replant new ones every spring, waiting until average daytime temperatures rise above 65 degrees.

Water lilies are vigorous growers, so choose a small variety that won't quickly blanket the surface and bunch over the container sides. Most water lilies need at least 4 to 6 hours of full sun each day; if your garden receives less than that, choose a variety that tolerates more shade.

After you purchase a lily plant, don't let it dry out; keep it in water until you are ready to plant it, and mist it during planting. You can buy a special planting pot from the plant supplier if you like, but a cut-down black plastic pot or a small dishpan works well. Fill the planting pot to within 1 inch of the top with un-improved heavy garden soil (peat, moss, and ground bark will encourage algae) mixed with 1 pound of granular controlled-release fertilizer or a fertilizer designed for water lilies. Remove any old leaves from the plant.

HARDY LILY

TROPICAL LILY

To plant a hardy lily, place the plant in the pot so that the growing tip is centered on the soil surface and its other end is sunk firmly at a 45-degree angle into the soil (left). Plant a tropical lily in the center of the pot so that its entire crown is above the soil line (below left); no part of the stems should be buried.

Water the planting pot thoroughly and cover the soil surface with clean gravel or pebbles to help prevent the soil from drifting out of the pot (or fish from nosing it out). Submerge the planting pot in the water garden container to the depth recommended for the lily variety. If you like, raise the pot on clean bricks initially, then gradually lower the pot as the lily grows. Fertilize the lily regularly with specially formulated lily fertilizer tabs, pushing them deep into the pot so that the fertilizer doesn't immediately leach into the water (and encourage algae).

ADDING OTHER AQUATIC PLANTS

Besides floating plants and water lilies, there are two other major categories of aquatic plants: marginals and oxygenating plants.

Marginals prefer to grow in the water margins, in the shallows, with their foliage in the air and their roots submerged in 2 to 6 inches of water. Most aquatic plants—including water clover *(Marsilea mutica)* and water hawthorn *(Aponogeton distachyus)*—are marginals. Plant one in a pot, following the same general planting instructions described for water lilies (above), but use no fertilizer. Choose a small pot if you want to contain the plant's growth; use a large one if you want it to grow vigorously. You can place the pot on a pond shelf or set it in the pond on a pedestal of clean bricks or stones. Do the same if you are making a water garden in a deep container. In a shallow container, place the plant pot on a bed of gravel or pebbles.

Oxygenating plants grow entirely submerged in the water, like the waterweeds in natural streams. Add a few oxygenating plants to any kind of water garden and you'll

SACRED AND FRAGRANT

Musky-scented sacred lotus *(Nelumbo nucifera),* revered by Buddhists, are as easy to grow as hardy water lilies if you have a warm-summer climate and a little bit of patience. They bloom in summer, usually the second summer after planting, once the water temperature has been at about 80 degrees for a few weeks. When the petals drop, the flower center forms an ornamental seedpod.

Choose a miniature variety, such as 'Momo Botan', and place the water garden where it will receive at least 6 hours of sun each day. Plant sacred lotus in the same way as a hardy water lily, but use a larger planting pot and feed more heavily. Like the hardy lily, sacred lotus will survive in the bottom of the water garden through the winter as long as the water around it doesn't freeze. (If it is likely to freeze, remove the rhizome and store it wrapped in moist sand in a cool place indoors.)

Types of Water Garden Plants

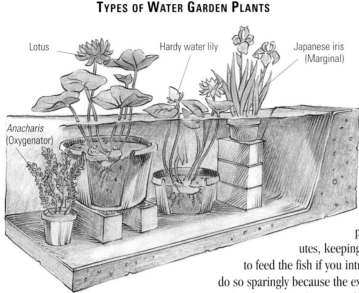

Lotus

Hardy water lily

Japanese iris (Marginal)

Anacharis (Oxygenator)

have less algae, because oxygenators absorb the nutrients in the water, effectively starving the algae. Aquarium sections of pet stores are good sources of oxygenators. Common ones include Canadian pondweed *(Elodea canadensis)* and eel grass *(Vallisneria americana)*. Plant a bunch in a small pot, using unamended heavy soil and no fertilizer; then water thoroughly, spread gravel or pebbles over the soil surface, and place the pot on the bottom of the water garden.

Adding fish

Mosquito fish *(Gambusia)* and the unexotic types of goldfish are the easiest fish to keep in a water garden. To acclimate the fish before releasing them from their plastic bag, float the bag on the water for about 20 minutes, keeping it shaded from hot sunlight with a cloth. There's no need to feed the fish if you introduce just two or three in a large bowl; if you feed them, do so sparingly because the extra fish waste will encourage algae. Besides providing life and movement to the water, fish contribute to the ecological balance of a water garden by eating mosquito eggs and algae.

Keeping the water clear

Algae is a vigorous water plant; like other plants, it will thrive when abundant warmth, light, and nutrients are available. To contain its growth without resorting to algicides (which don't prevent algae from returning immediately), keep the water as free of nutrients as you can. That means keeping fish waste and leached plant fertilizer to a minimum, and removing plant debris from the water before it decomposes.

Placing plants in the water—especially large-leafed plants, such as lilies, or spreading floating plants, such as water fern *(Azolla)*—makes less light available for algae growth. The plants also use the nutrients in the water, so less is available to the algae. Oxygenating plants absorb nutrients very efficiently, which makes them an important element in a strategy to combat algae. Fish can help, too, because they feed on algae. If you do decide to use an algicide, first check the product's effect on wildlife.

Keep mosquito larvae from hatching in the water by adding a small amount of the biological control *B. t. israelensis* (available in doughnut rounds, sometimes called mosquito dunks) or let fish feed on them.

Adding a simple fountain

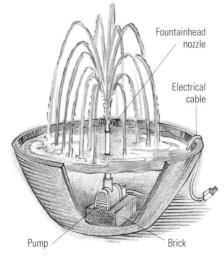

Fountainhead nozzle

Electrical cable

Pump

Brick

You can add a fountain to a water garden by screwing a fountainhead nozzle onto a water garden pump and submerging the pump so that the nozzle sits just below or just above the water surface. Placed below the water, a nozzle makes a low bubbler fountain like a spring; placed above, it makes a jet or a fancy spray pattern, depending on the nozzle type. To get it in the right position, rest the pump on clean bricks or concrete blocks or place it inside a camouflaging pile of pebbles. Take the pump's electrical cable out over the side of the water garden, under the leaves of a plant. For safety's sake, bury the cable and plug it into a properly installed GFI outlet.

A few simple solar-powered fountains are available consisting of a floating disk that contains solar panels and a small pump. When heat activates the panels, the pump sends a spray of water into the air. To make a wall fountain, see page 89.

MAKING A PEBBLE FOUNTAIN

In a pebble fountain, water rises from a reservoir through a fountainhead nozzle on a pump, spills over a tray of pebbles, and trickles back down to the reservoir.

Make the reservoir with a black liner, a preformed pond shell, or any kind of watertight container that is at least 15 inches deep. The reservoir can be just 18 inches wide or as much as 3 feet wide or even wider. If the reservoir is small, you'll need to remember to fill the reservoir frequently during hot or windy weather to ensure the water level never drops below the pump. In a site that's always windy, choose a low, bubbling fountainhead so the water doesn't fly away in the wind.

Dig a hole for the reservoir and set it in place. Place the pump in the reservoir on top of a clean brick, so the silt that collects on the reservoir bottom won't enter the pump. Fit a rigid extension pipe to the pump outlet and screw the fountainhead onto the top of the pipe. The fountainhead should just clear the top of the reservoir. If necessary, trim the extension pipe or raise the pump to reach the correct height. Take the electrical cable out over the edge of the reservoir in the direction of the GFI outlet.

Cut a piece of strong wire mesh to fit over the reservoir, overlapping the surrounding area by at least 6 inches. If necessary, cut a hole in the mesh to make room for the fountainhead. Position the mesh over the reservoir, then cut a square out of the mesh, big enough to put your hand through comfortably, so that you can reach the pump to adjust the water flow or clear the filter screen. Cover the hole with a larger square of mesh that won't sag into the hole once it's covered with pebbles.

Fill the reservoir with water. Place a few large pebbles on the edges of the wire mesh to hold it in place, then cover the rest of the mesh with pebbles. Mark the access to the pump with a few differently colored or glass pebbles. Turn on the electricity and then check the jet spray. Adjust the water flow on the pump if necessary to ensure that the spray stays within the circle of stones and drips back into the water reservoir.

PEBBLE FOUNTAIN

To GFI outlet

Water reservoir

Pebbles

Wire mesh

Flexible liner

NATURAL SPLASHING

Birds come to water to drink, to cool themselves in summer, and to keep their feathers clean and fluffed up in winter to retain warmth. They'll linger longest at a birdbath that is off the ground and near shrubs or trees that offer a quick escape from cats and other predators. A wide bowl or dish 2 to 3 inches deep with sloping sides is best; birds like to wade into the water. The bottom of the bowl should be textured so it isn't slippery.

Install the birdbath so that the rim is perfectly level. Because birds love fresh water, refill the bowl frequently. If there's an irrigation line nearby, consider clipping an emitter to the back of the bowl.

WATER AND SAFETY

Water, still or moving, is a magnet to children. For safety's sake, make a water garden—even a shallow one—inaccessible to them. To prevent drowning, cover the water garden with sturdy wire mesh or secure mesh just below the water surface (plants will grow through the mesh if it's fairly wide).

The electrical cable attached to a fountain pump should be plugged into a properly waterproofed GFI outlet; where the cable crosses the garden, keep it safe from the sharp blade of a spade or a child's digging tool by running it through a 1-inch PVC pipe and burying the pipe in the ground. In a large water garden, include a step or log so a pet that enters the water can climb back out.

VEGETABLE GARDENS

You can grow a bountiful crop of vegetables in even a skinny strip of sunny ground if you prepare the soil well, plant densely, and grow whatever you can vertically, on a tepee or trellis. A raised bed is particularly useful in a small space; it solves all kinds of problems, from poor drainage to gophers.

WHAT AND WHAT NOT TO PLANT

Vegetables that produce high yields in very little ground space make the best candidates for a small vegetable garden. That rules out corn, melons, and some sprawling squashes, but includes Asian greens, spinach, carrots, lettuce, and herbs. To save ground space, grow vining plants such as beans, peas, and tomatoes on stakes, frames, or trellises. To further boost your harvest, plant quick-growing radishes, lettuce, and green onions among slower-growing crops and harvest them before they get crowded out.

PREPARING THE SOIL

Good soil preparation is essential for a bountiful harvest. If your soil has not been worked recently, turn it over thoroughly (preferably in fall, unless your soil is prone to erosion by wind or rainfall) and then, well ahead of planting time, blend in organic amendments and fertilizers. If your soil has good texture and has been gardened before, you can apply amendments and fertilizers and mix them into the soil without prior tilling.

Soil amendments come in many forms. Wood products such as sawdust and bark work well in clay soils; if you are using raw wood products, add nitrogen to the soil. Manures improve most soils; choose an aged manure, but go easy with steer or poultry manure because the salts in them can harm young plants. Peat moss is ideal for sandy soils, but many gardeners won't use it because it's a nonrenewable resource. Compost is one of the best soil amendments.

MAKING COMPOST

Recycling garden and kitchen waste in a composting pile produces in a couple of months one of the very best garden soil amendments at almost no cost. Following are a few composting guidelines.

Spread a layer of plant debris (leaves, weeds, or grass clippings) 6 to 8 inches deep on the ground or in a bin. Follow with 1- to 2-inch layers of manure (or a few handfuls of nitrogen-rich fertilizer), topsoil, and kitchen scraps (except meat, fat, and bones). Continue adding layers. Chop or grind large materials, such as big stems, into small pieces; mix fine materials, such as grass clippings, with coarser pieces.

Construct a pile 4 to 6 feet high. This amount will hold the heat necessary to help the waste materials decompose while allowing sufficient air to enter the pile and minimize odor. Keep the compost moist but not soggy; it should be about as wet as a squeezed-out sponge. During heavy rainfall, cover the pile with a plastic sheet. Turn the pile at least every 3 to 4 weeks to discourage odor and flies and to help the compost decompose evenly.

If necessary, add small amounts of nitrogen—from sources such as fresh manure, blood meal, or commercial fertilizers—to the layers periodically to keep the decomposition process going.

Compost is ready to use when it is very crumbly and the starting materials have decomposed beyond recognition, usually after 1 to 3 months.

COMPOST BIN

Four wood frames, covered with chicken wire and latched together at the corners, can be unlatched to turn and remove compost.

BENEFITS OF RAISED BEDS

Plants thrive in raised beds filled with new soil. The drainage is good; the soil warms faster than ground soil in spring, boosting the growth of your plants; and, because you don't have to leave room for rows, you can place plants close together and thus reap a more bountiful harvest. Raised beds are the solution if your garden soil is too acid or alkaline for certain plants. They can also solve a gopher or mole problem: simply line the bottom of the beds with wire screening.

Raised beds can be made of many materials—brick, concrete, stone, logs, stakes, or railroad ties. If you are using lumber, avoid pressure-treated wood and new railroad ties; these materials contain toxins, and although it's not been proved that they affect the plants, it's best to be on the safe side.

Make a bed any length, but build it no more than 4 feet wide so you can reach the middle easily from either side. The height should allow for a soil depth of at least 12 to 18 inches. If you plan to use the edges of the bed for sitting, a comfortable height is 18 to 24 inches; a comfortable height for gardening from a wheelchair is about 16 inches. Leave room for a wheelbarrow between neighboring beds.

For vegetables and flowers, fill your raised beds with a rich, light soil mix, such as equal parts peat moss, compost, and topsoil. Remember to replenish the soil with compost or other organic soil amendments each time you replant the bed.

THE FRENCH INTENSIVE WAY

The French intensive method of planting vegetables produces the biggest harvests and arguably the best-tasting ones. Start by preparing the ground thoroughly, double digging it (digging down two spade depths and mixing amendments into both levels) and incorporating organic matter and sand to make a planting mix that's approximately one-third organic matter, one-third sand, and one-third original garden soil.

Mark out 3- to 5-foot-wide planting beds so they run north-south (make beds just 1½ feet wide for crops grown on vertical supports). Apply a complete fertilizer or organic source of nutrients, then rake the soil in each bed into a mound that is highest in the center.

Sow or plant crops close together in blocks rather than rows so that at almost all stages of growth, the leaves completely shade the soil and conserve soil moisture. Plants that produce over a long season and tolerate regular thinning are the best choices for a French intensive garden. Consider Asian greens, beets, carrots, leeks, lettuce, mustard greens, radishes, spinach, turnips, and Swiss chard. As the vegetables mature, thin them repeatedly, and take the thinnings to the salad bowl.

BUILDING A RAISED BED

1   For a 4-by-10-foot bed, first nail 4-foot-long 2 by 10s to 3-foot-high 4-by-4 corner posts. Use naturally decay-resistant redwood or cedar heartwood and galvanized nails.

2   Nail the 10-foot lengths to the corner posts. Work on level ground so that the bed is as square as possible.

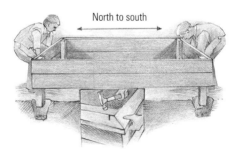

3   Set the bed right side up and orient it from north to south so both sides get equal sun. Insert the corner posts into predug 16-inch-deep holes. Level the soil underneath, if necessary. Cap the top with surfaced (planed smooth) redwood 2 by 6s, with ends cut at a 45-degree angle (see inset).

4   Place 3 to 4 inches of new soil in the bottom of the bed and mix it into the ground to aid drainage. Then fill the bed with a rich, light soil and soak it before planting. This 20-inch-deep raised bed holds about 2½ cubic yards of soil.

DOUBLE FEATURES

The most delightful and ingenious small gardens put every element to work in more ways than one. Decorative accents double as seating or mask noise, and structural elements such as paving and walls become precious growing areas for more plants.

FLOWER-FILLED FLOORS AND WALLS

Paths, patios, and walls can be designed to double as planting areas. Many types of plants will grow in the cracks between stones and bricks or up through gravel. Plant self-seeding annuals or perennials near a gravel path or patio, and chances are they'll spread into the paving. They'll also take hold between bricks and flagstones if the joints aren't mortared. Water as necessary to keep them growing luxuriantly.

Gaps of 2 inches between paving stones are sufficient for plantings of small creeping ground covers, such as blue star creeper (*Laurentia fluviatilis*, also known as *Isotoma fluviatilis*) and chamomile (*Chamaemelum nobile*); for the most walked-on parts of the paving, choose sturdy plants that will take foot traffic. Select young plants or tear larger clumping plants into small rooted pieces, fill the spaces with amended topsoil to ½ inch below the tops of the stones, insert the plants between the stones, tamp the soil firmly, and keep the plants well watered until they are established. If the plants fail, try sowing seeds in the gaps. Bulbs can also be planted in the gaps between paving, but keep them to the edges of the path or patio unless it's your intention to make people slow down and step around them when the bulbs are in bloom.

Seeds are the best way to start plants in the crevices of existing stone walls. Scratch out as much rubble as you can without jeopardizing the stability of the wall, pack soil into the crevices, and press the seeds into the soil. Keep the seeds well watered. If you are building a stone wall, prepare places for plants after laying each course of stones: choose the largest gaps between stones; line them with sphagnum moss (to help keep the soil in place); fill the pockets with soil; and plant young plants, tamping the soil firmly. Spray water into the planted areas regularly.

PLANT PARTNERS

A tree or a shrub can double as a support for a climbing rose, a delicate clematis, or another vine. If you use a flowering host plant, choose a vine that flowers in a different season, or color-coordinate the two types of flowers if they'll bloom at the same time. Plant the vine at least 18 inches away from the base of the host. To start a vine growing on a tree, provide a temporary support, such as chicken wire or plastic mesh, on the lower part of the trunk; you can cut away the support after a year or two. To grow a vine on a shrub, tie the vine to a low branch until it begins to twine or ramble on its own. Bear in mind that if the tree or shrub is tall, the vine may grow out of the reach of pruners.

You can also squeeze bulbs into a perennial bed and bring the garden into bloom before the perennials have started to bud. In fall, after you've cut back the perennials, plant the spaces between them with spring-flowering bulbs. The bulbs will have bloomed by the time the perennials are making new growth, and when the bulb foliage dies back, it'll be hidden under the fresh foliage of the perennials.

BOULDER SEATS

A boulder with a flat top makes a natural accent and also a casual seat. Search for one that will place the sitting surface 18 to 24 inches above the ground, a comfortable height for most people. To look natural, permanent, and stable, the boulder needs to be settled into the earth rather than simply placed on top of it. Sink it so that its widest surface is just under the ground; then it seems to rise from bedrock. To save yourself trouble and expense, choose a boulder that won't require much burying.

Two or three boulders on either side of a path could make a gathering place (see the illustration on the facing page). On the edge of a patio, boulders become occasional seating or side tables. Also consider placing a group of boulders on a lawn or under a tree and laying a stone floor around them to tie the composition together.

WALL FOUNTAINS

A wall fountain makes a fine focal point, decorates a dull wall, and provides in very little space the soothing sounds and sparkle of splashing water. Many kinds are available in kit form, or you could make your own with any spout and water trough.

Stone masks and lion heads are popular spouts, but a simple metal or bamboo spout may be easier to incorporate into contemporary garden styles. A faucet makes a natural-looking water source in city gardens. Any kind of water bowl or basin will do for a trough. If it's large, it will catch most of the fountain water and you won't need to remember to keep refilling it as the water evaporates during hot or windy weather. You can also raise the water reservoir closer to the fountain so there's less risk of the water being blown in a breeze completely off course into the garden.

The mechanics of a wall fountain are simple: water rises through a pipe (a length of flexible tubing) from a pump in the trough up to the spout, and spills back down to the trough. If you are building the wall that the fountain is to be mounted on, you can take the water delivery pipe behind the wall so it's out of sight. If the wall is already built or if it's a boundary wall, the pipe will have to go up the face of it, but you can hide it by planting a vine around the fountain or placing a tall water plant in the trough.

The pump's electrical cable needs to be plugged into a nearby GFI outlet (a proper waterproof outdoor electrical outlet). The simplest arrangement, shown below, is to take the cable out over the rim of the trough, hiding it under the foliage of a water plant or a garden plant trailing over the rim. Alternatively, you can raise the trough on bricks, concrete blocks, or a stone slab and take the cable out through a hole drilled in the base of the trough and then on to the GFI outlet; once the cable is in place, seal the hole with silicon caulking.

To assemble a fountain like this one, attach the mask to the wall with screws; if it's a heavy piece, first insert expanding anchors into the wall and thread the screws into the anchors. A mask usually looks best below eye level. If you are taking the water delivery pipe up the face of the wall, mount the mask a little away from the wall, on wood spacer blocks if necessary, to allow room for the pipe to pass behind it.

Place the pump in the reservoir on top of a clean brick, so the silt that collects on the reservoir bottom won't enter the pump. Attach the water delivery pipe to the pump and take it up behind the mask into the spout. Where the pipe enters the mask, attach a right-angle connector, as shown, so the pipe doesn't kink.

Finally, fill the trough with water, plug the electrical cable into the GFI outlet, and adjust the water flow so that the water returns reliably to the reservoir. Watch the water level in the trough on windy days; it mustn't fall below the water intake on the pump.

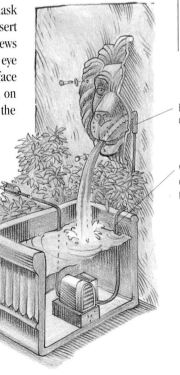

Right-angle connector

Water delivery pipe

FUNCTIONAL ART

In a small garden created by landscape architect Topher Delaney and artist and craftsman Pedro Castillo, art doubles as seating, and concrete walls and paving double as decorative objects. Hedges and flowers would have swallowed the tiny amount of floor space here at the end of a pool, but the whimsical ceramic bench and playfully colored and shaped concrete floor (note the pinkish purple grout) and wall make the pool edge a distinctive and usable terrace.

PLANT SALVAGE

Overgrown, dense planting destroys the scale of a small garden and creates too much shade. Here are ways to slim down tangled vines and pare back old shrubs, hedges, and trees so the plants are once again handsome and there's more light and space on the garden floor.

PRUNING CUTS

Thinning   Heading

WHAT TO RESTORE

Most experienced small-space gardeners have learned when not to try to rescue a plant. Sometimes, the plant choice was poor: for example, a vine that requires constant trimming to keep it looking attractive in a small garden. Likewise, some shrubs and hedge plants are simply too large for a small space; you could cut them to the ground, but they'll grow back just as large one day. Some trees are too tall, broad, and dense, and they may cast deep shade across the only area large enough to place a sitting area. Pruning may help, but be careful about accepting partial or temporary solutions. In a small garden, where every square yard is precious, it's sometimes better to pull a plant—even a tree—and replace it with a more suitable one.

RESTORING AN OLD VINE

To restore an old vine to a size that suits the space, first determine whether it's a clinging vine (see page 66). Clinging vines attach to surfaces by means of suction disks or aerial rootlets. Restoring them is slow work because you have to yank loose all the attachments before you can prune back the vines, and after that you may also have to clean and repair the surface. If you have a clinging vine that isn't too far out of bounds, just cut away growth that threatens to overrun a doorway or window and trim growth that juts out from the surface. If it's way out of bounds, and especially if the surface is in need of repair, consider removing the vine entirely, to save yourself any more trouble.

Other types of vines are easier to restore. Vines such as wisteria, which form a sturdy framework of woody stems and laterals, can be pruned back to their basic structure. Others, such as jasmine, have weak stems and no real structure to work with; to make these vines manageable, thin out entire stems rather than just heading them back (thinning produces less regrowth). Untangle overgrown stems as best you can in order to make the cuts, but if the stems are very tangled, just snip through sections of them.

If the base of a vine is bare of leaves, cut off some old stems to promote leafy young growth lower down. You can also head back shoots at the bottom of the vine, which will encourage them to branch. If the vine is flowering only at the top, prune out the older stems. If your vine is a big tangled mess and full of dead wood, skip the delicate pruning: leave any young shoots near the base of the vine; otherwise, before spring growth begins, cut the whole vine low to the ground and retrain the new growth that emerges.

To keep your restored vine looking pretty, assess it annually. Most vines can be pruned in winter, during their dormancy; if a vine grows rampantly, prune it in summer as well.

SALVAGING OLD SHRUBS

Many shrubs that send up stems, or canes, from the roots—including glossy abelia, berberis, butterfly bush *(Buddleia)*, flowering quince *(Chaenomeles)*, forsythia, hydrangea, mahonia, mock orange *(Philadelphus)*, and spiraea—can be restored by cutting the whole plant low to the ground before new spring growth begins. On shrubs that produce canes but don't respond well to severe pruning, spread the pruning over several years. The first year, don't prune at all; just fertilize and water the plant well to make it as healthy as possible. During the next 3 years, remove about a third of the oldest wood annually, cutting the stems to the ground.

TOP-PRUNING

Other shrubs form a framework of branches rather than sending up new canes from the base. These shrubs—which include most evergreen shrubs and a few deciduous ones, such as the deciduous hollies *(Ilex)*, winged euonymus *(Euonymus alata)*, and witch hazel *(Hamamelis)*—cannot be cut back to the ground if they've become overgrown; you must prune the tops to rejuvenate them. Over several years, head back selected branches severely to force new growth and make the plant smaller. Keep in mind that some shrubs will sprout new growth from leafless branches, but others won't. (For the best time and way to prune an individual plant, check Sunset's *Pruning* book or ask a knowledgeable nursery employee.)

TRANSFORMING A SHRUB INTO A TREE

A tall shrub with one or more strong, upright stems and a framework of branches can be "limbed up" into a small tree, which will create room for other plantings below it and a much lighter look in a small space. If the shrub is already mature, choose a healthy, well-placed trunk or trunks from the available upright stems and cut any others to the ground. Then remove the low branches on the trunks up to the height where you want the tree canopy to begin, and thin out any superfluous branches in the crown to make your tree more attractive. For a younger shrub, remove the branches gradually, over several years, because the longer the lower branches are left on, the stronger and thicker the trunks will be.

Shrubs often limbed up include callistemon, camellia (see "Aerial Camellia Hedge" on page 65), winged euonymus, holly, lilac *(Syringa)*, oleander *(Nerium oleander)*, osmanthus, privet *(Ligustrum)*, witch hazel, large rhododendrons, and some viburnums.

RENOVATING A HEDGE

One of the most common problems of an old hedge is a leggy, leafless bottom; to correct this, cut back the top growth severely to stimulate branching at the bottom. To avoid legginess on a formal or semiformal hedge, shape the hedge so that it's wider at the bottom than at the top so sunlight reaches the lower branches.

If your formal or semiformal hedge has developed holes or bare spots, you can try "pluck pruning"—cutting into the hedge to let light reach the interior, thus encouraging new growth. Bare spots may have been caused in part by removing the entire flush of new growth each year. Help prevent a recurrence by leaving ¼ inch of new growth when trimming the hedge.

For overgrown, rangy, or ratty-looking hedges, the solution varies depending on the formality of your hedge and the pruning technique recommended for the specific plants (see "Salvaging Old Shrubs" on the facing page). With an informal hedge, you can tend to each plant individually, rejuvenating only those that require it. With a formal or semiformal hedge, treat the hedge as a unit. If the plants will tolerate severe pruning, you can cut the hedge to the ground and let it grow back. This treatment is often used for old privet hedges. If you don't want to lose the screening your hedge provides, you can try cutting one side of the hedge back severely, close to the main stems if necessary, and do the same to the other side the next year.

MATURING GRACEFULLY

If you have a tree that's become too dense or large for its space, don't be tempted to top it (saw off its top branches), because topping will ruin the appearance of the tree forever—and it won't reduce the tree's height for long. Instead, hire a good arborist, who will scale back the tree by thinning it and by using a procedure called drop crotching to preserve the tree's natural shape.

Some shrubs and trees do not respond well to severe pruning. For example, once the branching framework of a flowering cherry tree has been established in the first years, the tree should be pruned as little as possible to avoid triggering a rash of new shoots that can spoil the tree's graceful lines. If you are planning to plant a flowering cherry, check the mature horizontal spread and height of each variety.

Every obstacle you are likely to face in landscaping a small garden has confronted other gardeners of small spaces before. Street noise, poor views, awkward spaces, only so much money to spend — these are familiar challenges. But there's no reason to be daunted. Chances

DESIGNING AROUND
OBSTACLES

are, you don't have the worst combination of obstacles in your yard, and other gardeners and garden designers have found ways of getting around even the toughest ones.

In this chapter, you'll find advice on everything from improving the soil so your plants grow well to reducing the dominating effect of high walls. You'll learn how to keep deep shade or strong wind off your patio so you can sit there in comfort, as well as how to address a lack of garden style. Lack of time is also taken on, with labor-saving suggestions to help you enjoy the time you can spend in the garden.

Struggling against constraints brings rewards. You become knowledgeable about the possibilities for masking the bad and tricking the eye into seeing only the good. The final reward is a garden that's beautiful, comfortable, and distinctive in style — an enviable garden that apparently had no obstacles at all.

A slit of water and long strips of ground cover, paving, and trees on either side of it dramatically emphasize the length of a small, narrow yard.

Design: Sam Williamson

COMMON PROBLEMS

One of the keys to making a garden beautiful is knowing what problems need to be overcome. Refer to these pages for help identifying obstacles that are common in landscaping small spaces, and experiment with the suggested solutions until you've corrected each one in your garden.

A clear barrier, just a few feet high, retains views from this deck while blocking wind.

POOR SOIL

If it remains untreated, poor soil can frustrate all your gardening efforts. Plants may grow hardly at all, show signs of disease, or fail.

For example, soil that is too clayey will drain poorly, causing water to pool around the roots and plants to suffocate. You can test for poor drainage by digging a hole 12 to 24 inches deep and filling it with water. If the hole does not empty in 24 hours, drainage is poor. Conversely, soil that is too sandy will drain too quickly, flushing away nutrients and letting plants dry out. Generous amounts of organic matter such as compost, composted manure, wood shavings, or ground bark will improve the soil drainage in either case. To get the best results,

Gardening in raised beds filled with a good soil mix is one way to overcome the problem of poor soil.

add about 25 to 50 percent of the total soil volume you are amending. For example, to amend soil to a depth of 6 to 8 inches, work 2 to 4 inches of organic matter into it. To make your own compost, see page 86.

If adding organic matter to clayey soil doesn't help, you may have an impervious layer of hard soil or clay below the topsoil, called hardpan, that does not allow water to drain through. A landscape contractor may be able to break up a thin layer of the hardpan with special equipment or may recommend subsurface drainage. A less expensive solution is to garden in raised beds (see page 86) or in mounds made of new topsoil.

You might have a different soil problem if native topsoil was removed or redistributed when your house was built. The soil that's left may be rocky, hard, or sandy and low in organic matter and nutrients. Adding organic matter will help improve the soil if it's not too poor, but often the best solution is to bring in new topsoil that's as close as possible to your native soil. Put it down in layers, tilling each layer into the ground.

As a matter of course, you might want to conduct a soil test. A soil test will tell you the soil pH (acidity or alkalinity) and can also reveal nutrient deficiencies in the soil. In some states, county cooperative extension offices can test your soil or direct you to commercial soil laboratories that can. Simple soil-test kits are also available from nurseries.

Sometimes the best information about soil conditions comes from neighbors and local nurseries. Ask about the native soil and learn not only about its problems but also what plants grow well in spite of them. Discovering the plants that will be happy in your poor soil is a simpler task than altering the soil.

NO SHELTER FROM WIND

Although gentle breezes bring a sense of nature into a garden, strong gusts make it unlikely people will stray far from the house. Heavy winds can also damage plants or cause soil erosion.

Protect the sitting areas in the garden first, so there's somewhere pleasant to linger outside; other areas may not need it, or not to the same degree. Consider a windbreak of trees and shrubs, a solid screen or fence, or a combination of the two.

Trees and shrubs planted close together and perpendicular to the wind direction can reduce wind by up to 50 percent, depending on the density and height of the plants. The protection is most effective close to the windbreak; it becomes significantly reduced at a distance about four times the height of the tallest tree.

A simple solid screen or fence provides complete wind protection but for a shorter distance, roughly equal to the height of the barrier, and at that point there are usually strong gusts of wind. You can increase a barrier's protection by adding baffles to the top that are angled into the wind, or by adding a louvered screen, which will diffuse the wind and offer good protection another 6 feet or so from the barrier.

In the windiest areas of the garden, choose plants that are tough enough to withstand wind. More delicate plants might thrive in the shelter of trees and large shrubs. Properly stake and tie plants, especially newly planted trees. To help them get established, make temporary windbreaks with burlap or shade cloth supported on a sturdy frame and apply water close to the ground, using drip irrigation, soaker hoses, or bubbler sprinkler heads. (Avoid watering with overhead sprinklers because the wind will blow the water away.) Set container plants in protected areas or water them frequently.

OUTSIDE NOISE

Noise from traffic or neighbors can ruin the privacy of a garden. It's hard to relax amid the ruckus of delivery trucks and radios.

A wall or fence or any other solid barrier, such as a berm of earth, helps to deflect noise. The most effective solution is a tall, solid wall. For a less expensive solution, consider a low wall, say, 3 feet high, with a berm behind it. Plants are not particularly good buffers of sound, but densely planted evergreen shrubs and trees are worth installing in combination with a solid barrier.

Masking unpleasant sounds with pleasant ones can also be effective. If you place a fountain in an outdoor sitting area, the gentle, soothing splashes of falling water will distract your attention from traffic sounds. (Don't try to drown traffic noise with a raging waterfall, because the sound of roaring water in a small yard can also be unsettling.) Wind chimes and birdsong are also good distractions.

Decide where in the garden you need the most privacy from noise (see page 22 for information on working with a privacy scale). Once you've done what you can to deflect and mask the noise, check whether you can make the area more private in other ways. Even if there is no place out of earshot of the street, you can create a small secluded spot that feels a long way away from it (see pages 48–51).

The sound of water tumbling from a fountain into a pool distracts the ear from unpleasant noise.

LONG, NARROW STRIP

A long, narrow strip of garden can look niggardly and uninviting; the eye travels quickly through and out of the space. Because a narrow strip is often at the side of a house, it is often also shady, which can make the space even more unattractive.

The most common solution is to break up the strip into a series of smaller areas and to position plants so that there's no straight view through. For example, at the start of the strip, you might make a mini-courtyard with chairs and wall-to-wall paving (see the photograph at the top of page 96); if possible, lay the paving so the lines run across the space, to emphasize its width. The middle section of the strip might be a path that

A mini-courtyard with distinctive paving breaks up a long, narrow strip of garden space.

Tall plantings and a soft-edged patio turn a square yard into a sanctuary (top). A pond joins two sections of an L-shaped garden (bottom).

weaves through the space, between shrubs that hide the walls. At the end of the strip might be another open area. Plant and decorate the areas differently to give a distinctive feeling to each.

Another solution is to play up the linear geometry of the shape and not attempt to disguise it at all (see page 92). A path might run down the center of the strip, with matching flowers or trees on both sides. You might try to make the strip even longer by continuing the path and symmetrical plantings through an open area at the start or end of the strip. If you narrow the path slightly at the far end, it will appear longer. You could also place mirrors on either side of the path to reflect the plantings and create the illusion that the space continues, but place them out of the line of the path or you'll see yourself walking toward them. A trompe l'oeil, or mural, can also expand the sense of space in a narrow strip. If your strip is shady, see "Too Much Shade," on page 99.

SQUARE YARD

A square yard can feel dull because a square is a static shape. Unless you introduce some dynamism and movement, people may not be inclined to spend time in your garden.

One approach is to bring diagonal lines into the garden. Run a path or a long patio diagonally across the square to a focal point in one corner to encourage people to step out into the garden and investigate what lies at the end of it. Then build a space (a patio or path) off the diagonal to create the sense of a second destination in the garden. If the garden is flat, you might make it more interesting by grading it so that you can create a couple of steps in the path or into the second space. Dynamic diagonal patterns are good choices for paving and fences in square yards.

A different solution is to take advantage of the static nature of the space and create a sanctuary there. Make a circle, an ellipsis, or another soft shape inside the square and plant the edges with screening plants to make the garden very sheltered (left). Decorate the garden richly, with fragrant and choice plants, and place objects of interest—bowls of water and pebbles, statues, special plants in special containers—on the perimeter so people can explore a little if they so choose.

L-SHAPED YARD

One part of an L-shaped yard is often wasted; from the entrance to the yard, people can see only one leg of it, so they never go to the other one. If the legs are narrow, the garden may also have the same problems as a long, narrow strip (see page 95).

To make use of your whole yard, in the corner of the L place a focal point, such as a pond (left), an ornamental tree, a group of boulders or tall containers, or an arbor that covers the corner. This will have the effect of completing each space; the garden will no longer just drift off somewhere. The focal point will also draw people to the corner, where they'll discover the second part of the garden.

Treat each leg of the L as a separate space, and give each a distinctive character. For example, one leg might be a lawn or a dining courtyard and the other a vegetable garden or a shrub and flower garden with stepping-stones through it.

IRREGULARLY SHAPED YARD

People feel uncomfortable in places that seem arbitrary or left over from other spaces. A long, tapered garden seems awkward in this way, as do pieces of garden between buildings or garden structures.

The solution is to form a regular shape within the irregular boundaries. For example, if the garden is shaped like a piece of pie, place a screen or an arch across the middle of the space, and create rectangular or square lawns or patios on both sides of it. Hide the leftover, angled edges of the garden behind layers of loose shrubs, flowers, and vines. To make the rectangles or squares seem completely natural, center them on the back door of the house, the sitting-room window, or a major focal point in the garden.

In odd areas between buildings, do exactly the same: Mark out a regular shape (a circle, semicircle, rectangle, or square). Define the shape with paving, columns, containers of tall plants, trellises, or screens. Disguise any odd corners by hiding them behind billowing plants.

SLOPING YARD

Slopes are more interesting than flat ground, but they reduce the amount of usable outdoor living space. Dining and sitting areas need to be set on level ground, and paths are off-putting if they look steep.

Although terracing will provide the maximum amount of flat land, it's a labor-intensive project. Consider a more selective approach, creating level areas only where you need them most. If the house is on sloping ground, make a flat area around the house, where possible, so the hillside doesn't seem about to slide into the walls or the house about to slip down the slope. If the slope comes down to the house, push it back behind a low retaining wall (see page 73). If the slope drops away from the house, perhaps build a deck out over it.

Place a patio on the flat area close to the house if there's room or choose the flattest area elsewhere in the garden. (It needn't be a neat rectangle; it could curve out from the house and into the trees.) Orient the patio sideways, across the direction of the slope, to make the most use of level land. Cut into the slope to expand the patio area, but don't be tempted to build out from the slope onto fill unless you work with a landscape professional to secure the filled area first.

There are two options for paths on a slope. A path can be a stairway that goes straight up the slope to emphasize its drama. Alternatively, it can gradually weave up the slope, to take the bite out of the climb and to make the journey through the garden much longer. Steps can also be built into sloping paths. For a safe, leisurely walk, make sure the treads of any steps are at least 15 inches wide and the risers no deeper than 6 inches. Break up any single flight of steps more than 5 feet high with a large landing.

Add interest to a path by taking it into the shade of a tree and back out into the sunlight, around boulders or sweeps of dramatic plants, over or beside water, to a view if possible or a stunning substitute, such as a bower covered in fragrant roses. Because a tour of a sloping garden requires effort, make sure you create plenty of level places to rest along the way.

A semipaved patio aligned to the glass porch converts a small leftover space into a sitting area.

An elevated deck creates a flat outdoor living space off the house.

Continued >

Common Problems

Once you've designated where you need flat areas and paths, consider how you might make use of the sloping contours in the rest of the garden to highlight their natural forms. Perhaps you could build a dry creek bed to follow a dip through the garden or a waterfall to spill naturally off a ledge.

Pedestals, pots, and foliage at different heights break up the face of this high wall.

HIGH WALLS

High walls around a small garden can dominate it and make it feel like a box. The garden seems to shrink within such strong boundaries.

The solution is to break up the face of each wall in some way. For example, you might place vertical elements against it, such as a vine, a tree, an arch or arbor, and tall ornaments on tall pedestals, so the wall shows in pieces between those elements. And you might also place a raised bed or a tall planting trough in front of it so that instead of a 7-foot wall, you are now looking at a less intimidating 5-foot wall with a 2-foot wall in front of it.

Decorating the wall with pots or a trellis or wall fountain also takes the eye off the wall face; it becomes background to the ornaments. If the wall is painted a pale or bright color, you can make it recede by painting it a darker shade. You might pierce the wall (see page 24) if that's possible, or create a similar effect with a mirror (page 31). Or take the eye up out of the walled space by placing pots or ornaments on top of the wall.

POOR VIEWS

Unattractive views make it difficult to achieve a sense of spaciousness in a small garden because you can't borrow any beautiful elements in the surrounding landscape. If the views need to be hidden, you can lose precious gardening space to dense screens. A garden unconnected to the larger landscape may also feel isolated and lack a pleasant atmosphere.

Check first whether all the views really are poor. Perhaps one or two small glimpses out of the garden can be saved (see pages 22–25 and 28–31). A view does not need to be awesome. The top of a garden umbrella on a neighbor's deck will give the view through the shrubs on your deck more depth. A view of a busy street, if you frame a portion of it through foliage, may also be worth saving if you can watch the progression of fall color in the ginkgo trees there. Save as much of a sky view as you can because of the sense of limitless space it provides.

Hide views where necessary, but always opt for the least amount of screening that will work (see pages 64–71). Often it's enough to distract the eye from a poor view (see pages 36–39 and "High Walls," above). Where you need a screen, consider the viewing point: for example, several tall plants or a trellis judiciously placed on a patio will block an unattractive view more efficiently than a line of thick conifers around the garden boundary. Think scrim rather than solid barrier; the best screening in a small garden allows light and a pleasant breeze to travel through.

A view out of the garden was left open between two woven privacy screens on this tiny rooftop deck.

If dense screens are unavoidable, connect your garden to the larger world by setting out plants that mark the change in seasons or that attract butterflies and birds (see pages 40–43), or make the most of the garden's isolation and develop it into a sanctuary (see pages 48–51).

TOO MUCH SHADE

Too much shade makes a garden uninviting. Most people love sunlight, as long as it's not too hot, and won't choose to walk or sit in darkness. Deep shade can be particularly problematic in a garden.

Except in hot-summer climates, try to make at least the areas immediately around the house doors sunny so that people will arrive at the house in welcoming sunlight and walk out from it with the same sense of delight. If trees or vines cast heavy shade, thin them if it's feasible (see pages 90–91) and catch reflections of light in a simple water garden (see pages 44 and 82).

An ideal patio has both shade and sunlight, allowing people to choose and change seats as the light moves. Dappled shade is prettier than dark shade and usually sufficient protection from heat and glare, so select patio trees with open branches and delicate leaves and trim any dense vines covering a patio arbor. If the patio is shaded by walls, try to create a view from the patio that is bathed in light; people are often content to sit in shade if they can see sunlight playing across the garden.

On shady walks, try to create pools of light near the path corners so you are always walking toward the light. For other ideas on catching the light in your garden, see pages 44–47. You don't need to banish darkness from the garden altogether; a small dark area can create an interesting, mysterious atmosphere (see page 50).

HODGEPODGE

A hodgepodge of different plants, paving materials, pots, furniture, and ornaments makes a visual chaos. The effect can be so off-putting that even the most beautiful items aren't appreciated.

The solution is to introduce some kind of order. When planning or remodeling the layout of a garden, consider what shapes will relate well to the lines of the house and garden and see if you can repeat one shape throughout the garden. A garden composed of rectangular spaces, for example, has a stronger sense of unity than one composed of a medley of forms.

If existing plantings are too various and fussy, you can simplify them (see pages 54–55) and organize them. For example, in a flower garden, decide to keep the roses and remove every plant that detracts from them, then give the roses a background that sets them off well, such as a green hedge. Dig up bulbs that are widely scattered among other plants and replant them into drifts. Some exquisite small gardens have a vast array of different plants that are unified by the repetition of one or two plants throughout the garden or by the similarity of the plants' leaf shapes or colors. Different plants can also be brought to order within loops or rectangles of boxwood.

Mismatched containers scattered haphazardly throughout the garden can also look chaotic. Instead, place pots in pairs as markers on either side of a door or a flight of steps, or as distinct, carefully arranged groups (see page 80). For example, pots of herbs could be displayed together in uniform containers on attractive staging, to create a focal point within the garden. Place ornaments in an orderly manner as well: make them a major focal point to a garden area or place them discreetly as small surprises (see pages 36–39). Continued >

A shady walk is enchanting if it leads into a bright space and a little light plays across the floor.

If your paving is diverse, consider ways of linking the materials. For example, border a gravel path leading off a deck with wood edging, make wood steps in the path, or set a wood planter or bench on it. When starting from scratch, choose a paving material that matches the house walls. House and garden then seem unified. For example, a concrete patio and path complement stucco masonry; a sawdust path and wooden deck look appropriate alongside a rustic wood cabin. Also, choose or arrange furniture so that it suits the style of each garden area (see pages 60–61).

Low trimmed hedges bring a satisfying sense of order to richly varied informal plantings.

LIMITED BUDGET

A small budget can seem like a major limitation to creating a beautiful garden. Fortunately, the elements of a garden that touch the senses most powerfully are not fancy benches or elaborate pots, but sunlight, a breeze, pretty shadows, water, and birdsong.

Nasturtiums sow themselves all over the garden from season to season.

If you're starting from scratch, direct your resources first toward creating a private, sheltered area so that you can immediately start to use the garden. Create screens with fast-growing plants, which are less expensive than fences, and find an old chair that you can take outside. Inexpensive paving materials, such as gravel, can be just as aesthetically pleasing as expensive cut stone. In fact, by choosing a simple material rather than an elaborate or sophisticated one, you are less likely to make an error in style. A compacted dirt floor could be perfect for a patio under a tree at the end of the garden. Spend any small amount of extra cash on details, such as a few flagstones at the threshold of the patio or a water bowl to catch reflections of the leaves unfolding in spring.

A truckload of soil amendment might also be a good idea, if you can afford it. If plants are healthy and growing well, the garden looks welcoming and successful. Consider planting inexpensive annuals such as love-in-a-mist *(Nigella damascena)* and Johnny-jump-up *(Viola tricolor)* that will reseed from year to year. A happy plant running wild is enchanting and gives a sense of unity to the garden, but be judicious about where and how many prolific self-seeders you place in a small space.

NO SENSE OF STYLE

One person's idea of landscape style may not be another's. Closely following the dictates of others on what is fashionable might not work for you. In fact, trying too hard to achieve a sense of "style" could leave you with a garden that appears overdecorated, with no sense of style at all.

Rather than copying someone else's tastes, consider what pleases you. What is your personal style? What do you like? In every decision you make about the garden, beginning with the shape of a patio, for example, think about what you find attractive and then check carefully whether it will work in your garden. Do you like the peacefulness of circles or dynamic zigzagging lines? Do you like the sound of gravel crunching underfoot or the tapping of shoes on smooth cut stone? Does the color of the gravel look good—to you—with the house color and the color of your roses? A sense of style will emerge from all these small decisions carefully attended to.

The process is frustrating at times (many desired things are best relegated to a fantasy garden). You love geometric lines, say, but they won't work on a slope; you love the sample of pink stone, but you know pink won't look good on a large scale. The trick to achieving a garden with style is to proceed inch by inch, with much deliberation, study, and restraint.

In the end, it's usually necessary to strip away all the unnecessary decorations and half-admitted mistakes, and to come to the decision that your garden, or at least each section of it, has just one main theme, one big idea. It will probably be something close to your heart or straight from your life, such as a collection of old shrub roses that remind you of a garden from years ago, or recycled glass that you discovered you could pick up for free from the industrial part of your town. This honest expression of personal style is more interesting to everyone than a hodgepodge of copied fashionable things.

An interest in succulents and recycled materials created this strong personal style.

Design: Jana Olson Drobinsky

NO TIME

A garden that isn't maintained makes both gardener and guests uncomfortable. The patio furniture may look romantic when littered with old bougainvillea petals, but if the plants appear uncared for, the atmosphere is depressing.

One way to keep up with garden maintenance is to install a garden that essentially takes care of itself, with large areas of paving, automatic irrigation, and tough evergreen shrubs. However, if you love to use a hose and to see the garden change dramatically with the seasons, that solution won't suit you. An alternative approach is to develop a garden that reduces the tasks you hate—pruning vigorous vines, perhaps—and includes mostly tasks you enjoy, such as raking oak leaves off a gravel path or deadheading roses with much-loved old pruners.

Excellent soil (see "Poor Soil" on page 94) and plants that are extremely well suited to your climate and conditions will get the garden off to an easy start. Installing mulch and an automatic irrigation system will reduce the need for weeding and watering. If you dislike sweeping and raking, avoid planting trees and shrubs that drop their fruits, flowers, and leaves messily. Choose plants that won't outgrow the space, unless you enjoy almost continuous pruning. Plan groups of a single type of plant; they are much simpler to maintain than a thousand different plants. And as the seasons change, make a mental note of the maintenance the garden needs—the fertilizer program, for example, but also one or two quick morning chores, like sweeping the fall leaves off the patio, to help ensure everyone's first impressions of the garden are always good.

You may long for an extremely low maintenance garden if the only time you go in the yard is to try to catch up with an endless list of chores. Occasionally, you can ignore the "have-tos" and "shoulds" and just relax and enjoy your garden. Bring your coffee and newspaper outside on a spring morning before heading off to work, move dinner to the patio to take advantage of a perfect summer evening, or spend part of a fall afternoon on a lounge, catching up on your reading while enjoying the first ripe apples. You may even fool yourself into puttering in the garden, just for fun.

Each different plant and object in the garden requires its own maintenance program. Repeating elements—a tree, a birdbath, an iris—results in a shorter list of chores.

It's at nurseries that a small garden feels smallest. Even if it has never occurred to you before, you may suddenly wish you had room for ground cover roses, heritage roses, and a rose arch—plus a big group of tropicals to start a new type of garden this year.

Shopping for
PLANTS

Instead of stocking the garden with plants you can't resist, set out for the nursery determined to be canny: to put together exquisite plantings that will work in your space. This chapter will help you get started. You'll find plants listed here that work particularly well for small gardens—the suggested trees, hedges, and vines, for example, all look good up close all year and won't outgrow their allotted spaces. You'll also find lists of bright-foliaged plants that will lighten up a shady area, and plants with soaring flower spikes to add height to a border.

Don't rush your decisions. Develop your ideas by collecting and studying foliage samples, color charts, and notes on what grows well in your neighborhood. Your real preference, once you've thought things through, might not be for roses but for plants that are lovely in every season.

A selection of dark- and bright-foliaged plants and a few decorative objects make an interesting display on the steps of an urban home.
Design: Suzanne Porter

TREES

Choose trees carefully for a small garden. The right choice will make the garden delightful for decades; the wrong choice, perhaps just a larger cultivar of the same species, may give you years of trouble. The following trees, many of them shrub-trees, are beautiful up close and in every season. They are relatively small; choose wisely between trees that will grow to 15 feet tall and those that will reach 25 feet.

ACER. Maple
HARDINESS VARIES. ☀ ◐ ◔ ● SUN OR PARTIAL SHADE, MODERATE TO REGULAR WATER. DECIDUOUS.

Choose the picturesque shrub-tree maples, not the large shade trees, which can grow fast to 100 ft. *A. japonicum* 'Aconitifolium' (fernleaf fullmoon maple), hardy to −10°F/−23°C, has leaves very deeply cut, almost to leafstalk, and orangish red fall color; it grows to 20 ft. Give it regular water. The leaves of *A. shirasawanum* 'Aureum' (golden fullmoon maple), −10°F/−23°C, open pale gold in spring and remain a pale chartreuse yellow all summer, then turn red in fall; it grows to 20 ft. Both maples need some shade in warm areas. *A. palmatum* (Japanese maple), 0°F/−18°C, is the most airy and delicate maple. The young spring growth is glowing red; summer's leaves are soft green; fall foliage is scarlet, orange, or yellow. Numerous varieties available, several with red or purple summer foliage. Grows slowly to 20 ft.

CHIONANTHUS RETUSUS. Chinese fringe tree
0°F/−18°C. ☀ ◔ ● SUN, MODERATE TO REGULAR WATER. DECIDUOUS.

Produces narrow, fringelike, white flower petals in lacy clusters; tree looks something like a tremendous white lilac when in bloom in late spring or early summer. Broad leaves turn bright to deep yellow in fall. Handsome grayish brown bark (sometimes golden on young stems). Grows to 20 ft. Can also be grown as a big, multistemmed shrub. Needs some winter chill.

CORNUS. Dogwood
−10°F/−23°C. ☀ ◐ ● SUN OR LIGHT SHADE, REGULAR WATER. DECIDUOUS.

Choose a species described as a shrub or small tree to about 20 ft. tall; large tree species can grow to 50 ft. *C. kousa* (kousa dogwood) has lustrous, medium green leaves that turn yellow or scarlet in fall and creamy white, slender-pointed flowers (actually bracts) with pink edges; it flowers in late spring or early summer, then produces red fruit that hangs below branches like big strawberries. *C. rutgersensis* (stellar dogwood) is an earlier-flowering hybrid between *C. kousa* and *C. florida* with red fall leaves; 'Stellar Pink' has pink bracts. *C. mas* (cornelian cherry) bears small, soft yellow blossoms on bare twigs in

TOP: *Acer palmatum* 'Ever Red'
BOTTOM: *Chionanthus retusus*

late winter or early spring, and shiny green leaves that turn yellow or red in fall among edible, bright red, cherry-size berries that attract birds; flaking, mottled gray-and-tan bark provides interest in winter.

EUCALYPTUS TORQUATA. Coral gum
22°F/−6°C. ☀ ○ ● SUN, SUPREMELY TOLERANT OF ARIDITY. EVERGREEN.

Slender, narrow tree to 15–20 ft. tall. Bears flower buds like little Japanese lanterns, from which open beautiful flowers of coral red and yellow, on and off all year. Light green to golden green leaves. Rough, flaky bark.

PRUNUS MUME. Japanese flowering apricot, Japanese flowering plum
0°F/−18°C. ☀ ◔ ● SUN, MODERATE TO REGULAR WATER. DECIDUOUS.

Longer-lived, tougher, more trouble-free than other flowering fruit trees. Blooms in winter; white or pink flowers are profuse, small, with clean, spicy fragrance. Fruit is small, inedible. Broad, oval leaves. Eventually develops into gnarled, picturesque 20-ft.-tall tree. 'Bonita' has semidouble, rose red flowers; 'Dawn' has large, ruffled, double pink blooms; 'Peggy Clarke' has double, deep rose flowers with extremely long stamens.

SORBUS TIANSHANICA. Turkestan mountain ash
0°F/−18°C. ☀ ◐ ◔ ● SUN OR LIGHT SHADE, MODERATE TO REGULAR WATER. DECIDUOUS.

Produces broad, flat clusters of white flowers in spring that develop into hanging clusters of bright red fruit in late summer or early autumn. Fruit persists after leaves fall; attracts birds. Fernlike foliage is finely cut into numerous leaflets. Has neat form; grows slowly to 16 ft. Needs some winter chill.

TRISTANIOPSIS LAURINA (TRISTANIA LAURINA)
30°F/1°C. ☀ ◔ ● SUN, LITTLE TO MODERATE WATER. EVERGREEN.

A small relative of eucalyptus with handsome glossy green leaves, clusters of small yellow flowers in late spring and early summer, and mahogany-colored bark that peels to show white new bark. Grows to 20–25 ft. Can also be grown as a tall shrub.

HEDGES

Choose a hedge that matches the purpose it will serve: for example, a dense, perhaps thorny barrier to keep pets in; a fine-textured evergreen hedge for a background; or loose, small, flowering plants to mark the edge of the lawn (see pages 64–66). Be careful not to buy a plant that grows too tall or broad. In the following list, a low hedge can be kept below 3 feet, a medium hedge below eye level; a tall hedge will grow above eye level.

BAMBOO
20°F/–7°C. ☼ ◐ ◒ ● SUN OR LIGHT SHADE, LITTLE TO REGULAR WATER. EVERGREEN, LOW TO TALL, INFORMAL.

Many kinds, some far too tall or fast-spreading for small spaces. Clumping bamboos have graceful arching stems and foliage that can look tropical paired with broad-leafed tropical plants, such as canna. A clumping kind won't spread far into surrounding soil, but contain it in small spaces. Running bamboos are generally taller and grow more or less vertical; they can spread rapidly. Many specialist varieties have striped or marbled stems (culms). Contain all running bamboos by planting in large pots or long flue tiles or by making 2- to 3-ft.-deep barriers around the plants with strips of galvanized sheet metal, 30-ml plastic, or poured concrete.

BUXUS. Boxwood, Box
0°F/–18°C. ☼ ◐ ◒ ● SUN OR SHADE, REGULAR WATER. EVERGREEN, LOW OR MEDIUM HEIGHT, FORMAL TO INFORMAL.

Widely used for small, dense, clipped hedges. When not clipped, growth is soft and billowing. Easy to grow; sprouts from bare wood when pruned. Several varieties, including compact dwarf kinds for edging.

CHAENOMELES. Flowering quince
–10°F/–23°C. ☼ ◒ ● SUN, MODERATE TO REGULAR WATER. DECIDUOUS, LOW TO TALL, SEMIFORMAL OR INFORMAL.

Many named varieties, some tall and upright, some low and spreading. All have showy early flowers (January in mild climates), shiny green leaves, and attractive angular branching patterns. Most are thorny; a few thornless varieties are available. Some bear quincelike fruit. Easy to grow. Prune in bud and bloom season.

FAGUS. Beech
HARDINESS VARIES. ☼ ◐ ◒ ● SUN OR PARTIAL SHADE, MODERATE TO REGULAR WATER. DECIDUOUS, MEDIUM TO TALL, FORMAL.

Glossy, dark green, dense foliage that colors yellow to reddish brown in fall, then turns brown and may hang on hedge well into winter. New foliage has a silky sheen. Several species available, including *F. sylvatica* 'Atropunicea' (often sold as 'Riversii' or 'Purpurea' or copper or purple beech), –10°F/–23°C, which has deep reddish or purple leaves.

TOP: *Buxus microphylla japonica*
BOTTOM: *Chaenomeles*

ILEX. Holly
HARDINESS VARIES. ☼ ◐ ● SUN OR PARTIAL SHADE, REGULAR WATER. EVERGREEN OR DECIDUOUS, LOW TO TALL, FORMAL TO INFORMAL.

Many species available, from foot-high dwarfs to tall screens. Choose small-leafed species, such as *I. vomitoria* (yaupon), hardy to 20°F/–7°C, for shearing into formal hedge; use larger-leafed types for semiformal or informal hedge. *I. aquifolium* (English holly), 10°F/–12°C, is the classic holly but not the best choice for eastern and midwestern gardens. *I. cornuta* (Chinese holly), 10°F/–12°C, has exceptionally large, bright red, long-lasting berries; the 'Burfordii' variety has a heavy fruit set and, like several hollies, is self-fertile so doesn't need male plants present to set fruit.

SPIRAEA
HARDINESS VARIES BY SPECIES. ☼ ◐ ◒ ● SUN OR PARTIAL SHADE, MODERATE TO REGULAR WATER. DECIDUOUS, LOW OR MEDIUM HEIGHT, SEMIFORMAL OR INFORMAL.

The shrubby spiraeas are best for small hedges; they typically grow knee-high and bear pink, red, or white flowers at branch ends in summer to fall. (Bridal wreath spiraeas are generally too tall and broad for small spaces.) Easy to grow. Many varieties have colored foliage.

TAXUS MEDIA. Yew
HARDINESS VARIES. ☼ ◐ ◒ ● SUN OR PARTIAL SHADE, MODERATE TO REGULAR WATER. EVERGREEN, LOW TO TALL, FORMAL TO INFORMAL.

Dark green conifer with small, soft needles and fleshy scarlet fruit instead of cones. Easily kept neat, dense, and small; can be cut back to bare wood and will resprout. Two popular hedging varieties are *T. media* 'Brownii', hardy to –10°F/–23°C, a compact, rounded plant to 4–8 ft. tall; and *T. media* 'Hicksii', –20°F/–29°C, which grows narrow and upright to 10–12 ft.

TEUCRIUM FRUTICANS 'COMPACTUM'. Bush germander
20°F/–7°C. ☼ ◐ ● SUN, MODERATE WATER. EVERGREEN, MEDIUM HEIGHT, FORMAL TO INFORMAL.

Silvery shrub to 3 ft. tall. Bears deep blue flower spikes at branch ends almost year-round if left unpruned or pruned lightly in late winter.

VINES

Many common vines, such as wisteria and passionflower, grow too large for a small space unless contained in a pot, and become too heavy for a simple trellis or a garden fence. Even if you want to smother a garden shed, consider a modest and delicate vine. The vines listed below are all twining vines except for the climbing rose, which needs tying. For more information on choosing a vine, see page 66.

CLEMATIS
HARDINESS VARIES. ☼ ● ROOTS NEED TO BE COOL, TOPS IN SUN; REGULAR WATER. DECIDUOUS.

Two hundred or so species available in huge range of sizes, from 8 to 40 ft. Flowers may be small and delicate, like those of *C. texensis*, hardy to −20°F/ −29°C; or huge, flat saucers, as in many of the hybrids. To reduce the need for restrictive pruning, avoid the very vigorous *C. montana* and evergreen *C. armandii*.

HARDENBERGIA
HARDINESS VARIES. ☼ ◑ ● SUN, PARTIAL SHADE IN HOT AREAS, MODERATE WATER. EVERGREEN.

Blooms during late winter and early spring, bearing long, slender clusters of sweet pea–shaped flowers. Grows at a moderate rate to 10 ft. Two species are available: *H. violacea*, hardy to 40°F/4°C, bushy, with deep green leaves and 5-in. sprays of violet, lilac, pink, or white flowers; and *H. comptoniana*, 37°F/3°C, more delicate, with vivid violet blue blossoms in narrow sprays to 6 in. or longer.

HIBBERTIA SCANDENS. Guinea gold vine
41°F/5°C. ☼ ◑ ● SUN OR PARTIAL SHADE, REGULAR WATER. EVERGREEN.

Handsome all year. Waxy, dark green leaves; 3-in.-wide lemon yellow blossoms that look like wild roses from spring to early fall. Shrubby. Grows fast to 10 ft. Recovers quickly from light frosts.

JASMINUM. Jasmine
30°F/−1°C. ☼ ◑ ● SUN OR PARTIAL SHADE, REGULAR WATER. EVERGREEN, SEMIEVERGREEN, OR DECIDUOUS.

Genus includes several fragrant vines with pinwheel-shaped flowers, either pure white or white tinged with pink or purple. *J. grandiflorum* (Spanish jasmine) and *J. officinale* (common white or poet's jasmine) are semievergreen in warmer climates, deciduous in cold areas. Both bloom in summer. *J. grandiflorum* can reach 15 ft.; *J. officinale*, 30 ft. Evergreen *J. polyanthum* grows quickly to 20 ft.; it blooms in late winter and spring, sporadically the rest of year. *J. nitidum* (shining or angelwing jasmine) is powerfully fragrant, blooms in late spring and summer, is evergreen in mild climates, grows to 10–20 ft.

TOP: *Clematis*
BOTTOM: *Lonicera japonica*

LONICERA. Honeysuckle
HARDINESS VARIES. ☼ ◑ ● SUN OR LIGHT SHADE, MODERATE WATER. EVERGREEN, SEMIEVERGREEN, OR DECIDUOUS.

Several species available, some too vigorous for small spaces. *L. brownii* 'Dropmore Scarlet', hardy to −20°F/−29°C, has deciduous blue green leaves and clusters of unscented tubular, red flowers that appear from early summer to frost; it grows to 10 ft. *L. heckrottii* (gold flame or coral honeysuckle), 0°F/−18°C, has blue green leaves that are deciduous in cold climates, semievergreen in mild climates, and lightly scented flowers that are bright coral pink outside and rich yellow within from spring to frost; it grows to 15 ft. *L. periclymenum* (woodbine), −10°F/−23°C, is evergreen in mild areas, deciduous elsewhere; it resembles the popular *L. japonica* 'Halliana' (Japanese honeysuckle) with its sweet-scented white flowers that age to yellow, but grows to 20 ft. rather than 30 ft. and won't smother other plants.

MANDEVILLA LAXA. Chilean jasmine
HARDINESS VARIES. ☼ ◑ ● SUN, PARTIAL SHADE IN HOTTEST AREAS, REGULAR WATER. DECIDUOUS.

Clusters of trumpet-shaped, white summer flowers produce heady fragrance, more like gardenia than jasmine. Grows to 15 ft. or more. An evergreen mandevilla, *M.* 'Alice du Pont', is too tender (hardy to 50°F/10°C) for most climates but makes an excellent container plant; red-throated, hot pink flowers appear from spring into fall.

ROSA. Rose
HARDINESS VARIES WITH SPECIES. ☼ ◑ ● SUN OR PARTIAL SHADE, REGULAR WATER. DECIDUOUS.

Roses classed as ramblers or natural climbers have thin, limber canes that are easily guided and tied into place; most flower only in spring, on vigorous plants that reach 15–25 ft. Roses classed as large-flowered climbers, climbing hybrid teas, climbing grandifloras, or climbing floribundas usually have thicker, stiffer canes and showier flowers, and grow 8–25 ft. or more. Consider also pillar roses (see page 67) and climbing species roses, including *R. banksiae* (Lady Banks' rose), an evergreen climber that grows vigorously to 20 ft. or more and bears large clusters of small yellow or white flowers in early to late spring.

ESPALIERS

A plant suitable for espaliering has a naturally arching form or pliant branches (see pages 78–79 for formal and informal training methods). The list below includes ornamental plants, but many fruit trees can also be espaliered, including apple and pear—the best candidates for geometric patterns—and citrus, Japanese persimmon, peaches, nectarines, apricots, cherries, and plums, for less rigid designs. Figs can be espaliered formally or informally.

ABUTILON. Flowering maple, Chinese bellflower, Chinese lantern
HARDINESS VARIES. ☼ ◐ ◗ ● SUN, PARTIAL SHADE IN HOT-SUMMER AREAS, MODERATE TO REGULAR WATER. EVERGREEN VINE-SHRUBS.

Fast-growing, rangy stems to 10 ft. tall. *A. hybridum*, hardy to 30°F/–1°C, has broad, maplelike leaves and bell flowers in white, yellow, pink, and red. Main blooming season is spring, but white and yellow forms may bloom almost continuously. Leaves of *A. megapotamicum*, 20°F/–7°C, are arrowlike; flowers resemble red-and-yellow lanterns; 'Variegata' has leaves mottled with yellow. *A. pictum* 'Thompsonii', 20°F/–7°C, is similar to *A. hybridum*, but foliage is strikingly variegated with creamy yellow, and the plant blooms almost continuously, bearing pale orange bells veined with red. All attract hummingbirds. Can be trained as standards.

CESTRUM ELEGANS (C. PURPUREUM). Red cestrum
41°F/5°C. ◐ ● PARTIAL SHADE, REGULAR WATER. EVERGREEN, SEMICLIMBING SHRUB.

Arching plant to 10 ft. tall or more with deep green oval leaves. Masses of showy, tubular, purplish red flowers appear in spring and summer, followed by red berries. 'Smithii' has pink flowers. Hummingbirds and warblers attracted to flowers, mockingbirds to berries.

HIBISCUS ROSA-SINENSIS. Chinese hibiscus, tropical hibiscus
50°F/10°C. ☼ ● SUN, REGULAR WATER. EVERGREEN SHRUB.

Glossy foliage; extremely showy flowers that last only a day but bloom continuously through summer. Many varieties available. Flower color ranges from white through pink to red, from yellow and apricot to orange. Height ranges from 4 to 15 ft. Choose a loose, open-branching variety, not the dense dwarf ones. Can also be grown as a standard.

LABURNUM WATERERI 'VOSSII'. Goldenchain tree
0°F/–18°C. ☼ ◐ ● SUN, AFTERNOON SHADE IN HOT AREAS, REGULAR WATER. LARGE DECIDUOUS SHRUB OR SMALL TREE.

Green bark; bright green, cloverlike leaves. In mid- to late spring, bears yellow, sweet pea–shaped flowers in hanging clusters like wisteria

TOP: *Cestrum elegans*
BOTTOM: *Pyracantha*

blossoms. Grows tall, to 15 ft. Graceful 'Vossii' is the only recommended variety for an espalier. Performs best in the Northeast and Pacific Coast states; grows poorly or fails in lower Midwest and lower South. Provide well-drained soil. If possible, remove seedpods; not only are they toxic, but a heavy crop drains the plant's strength.

OSMANTHUS FRAGRANS. Sweet olive
30°F/–1°C. ☼ ◐ ◗ ● SUN, AFTERNOON SHADE IN HOT-SUMMER REGIONS, MODERATE TO REGULAR WATER. EVERGREEN SHRUB.

Glossy oval leaves; tiny white flowers with powerfully sweet, apricot-like fragrance. Bloom heaviest in spring and early summer, but flowers appear sporadically throughout the year in mild-winter areas. Grows to 10 ft. or more. Can be trained as a small tree, hedge, or screen. *O. f. aurantiacus* has narrower, less glossy leaves; most of its crop of wonderfully fragrant orange flowers blooms in early fall.

PODOCARPUS
HARDINESS VARIES. ☼ ◐ ◗ ● SUN OR PARTIAL SHADE, MODERATE TO REGULAR WATER. EVERGREEN SHRUB OR VINE.

Good-looking foliage for screen or background; resembles that of yews *(Taxus)* but longer, broader, and lighter in color. Two species make good tall espaliers: *P. macrophyllus* (yew pine), hardy to 10°F/–12°C, with bright green leaves; and *P. gracilior* (often sold as *P. elongatus*, or fern pine), 40°F/4°C, with smaller leaves from glossy dark green to blue green or gray. Choose plants of *P. gracilior* grown from cuttings or grafts (plants grown from seed produce strong vertical growth unsuitable for espalier).

PYRACANTHA. Firethorn
HARDINESS VARIES. ☼ ● SUN, MODERATE WATER. EVERGREEN SHRUBS.

All species grow fast and vigorously and bear thick clusters of bright orangish red berries attractive to birds. For the most fruit, choose a naturally spreading shrub variety (some firethorns are ground covers) and prune only to check wayward branches. *P. fortuneana*, hardy to 10°F/–12°C, is a particularly good choice for a tall espalier (to 15 ft. tall, 10 ft. wide) because of its limber branches; its orange to coral berries last through winter. Can be trained as a formal espalier.

FALL AND WINTER INTEREST

Even in the dead of winter, a small garden can be worth exploring. The list below includes plants with striking displays of scarlet or gold fall and winter leaf color, showy violet berries, or brazen flowers that bloom and release a sweet fragrance in the bitter cold. An evergreen background makes them more stunning.

CALLICARPA. Beautyberry

HARDINESS VARIES. ☼ ☼ ◐ ◐ SUN OR LIGHT SHADE, MODERATE TO REGULAR WATER. DECIDUOUS SHRUBS.

Graceful, arching shrubs with small lilac summer flowers followed by tight clusters of small, round, lavender to violet purple fruits persisting into winter. Several species, from 3 to 8 ft. tall. *C. bodinieri,* hardy to 0°F/–18°C, grows to 6 ft. or more, with willowlike leaves that turn pink or orange to purple in fall; berries are violet.

CHIMONANTHUS PRAECOX (C. FRAGRANS, MERATIA PRAECOX). Wintersweet

10°F/–12°C. ☼ ☼ ◐ SUN OR PARTIAL SHADE, MODERATE WATER. DECIDUOUS SHRUB OR SMALL TREE.

Wonderfully spicy-scented, pale yellow blossoms with chocolate-colored centers last for many winter months, unless frosted. Tall, open, slow growing to 10–15 ft. tall and 6–8 ft. wide, with many basal stems. Keep smaller by cutting back during bloom, or remove excess basal stems and shape as a small tree. Can also be trimmed to within 1 ft. of ground in late winter if it becomes too large. Needs some winter cold.

EUONYMUS ALATA 'COMPACTA'. Winged euonymus

–20°F/–29°C. ☼ ◐ ◐ ◐ BEST FALL COLOR IN SUN BUT TOLERATES FAIRLY DEEP SHADE, MODERATE TO REGULAR WATER. DECIDUOUS SHRUB.

Dense, twiggy, flat-topped shrub to 6–10 ft. tall and a little narrower. Ornamental fall fruit and leaves: pink to red capsules open to reveal bright orange seeds; dark green leaves turn flaming red in sun, pink in shade. Young twigs have flat, corky wings. Makes good informal hedge. (Be sure to buy 'Compacta'; the species can grow to 20 ft. tall and wide.)

HELLEBORUS. Hellebore

HARDINESS VARIES. ◐ ● ◐ ◐ PARTIAL OR DEEP SHADE, MODERATE TO REGULAR WATER, EXCEPT AS NOTED. PERENNIAL.

Elegant evergreen shade plants with distinctive, nodding flowers. Flowers of *H. niger* (Christmas rose) start out white or greenish white and age to pink or purple; they appear sometime between December and early spring. Hardy to –30°F/–34°C; needs winter chill. *H. orientalis* (Lenten rose) flowers in late winter and early spring, bearing large blooms in greenish white, pink shades, or maroon, often with dark spots; self-sows freely. Same hardiness as Christmas rose but doesn't need freezing weather to succeed. *H. argutifolius* (*H. lividus corsicus,* or Corsican hellebore) reaches 3 ft. tall, twice the height of others; its light chartreuse flowers often appear in late fall in mild-winter areas. Foliage and flower buds hardy to 5°F/–15°C; tolerates some sun and drought.

HYDRANGEA QUERCIFOLIA. Oakleaf hydrangea

☼ ☼ ◐ SUN, SOME SHADE IN HOT-SUMMER CLIMATES, REGULAR WATER. DECIDUOUS SHRUB.

Broad, rounded, fast-growing shrub to 6 ft. tall with large, handsome, deeply lobed, oaklike leaves that turn bronze or crimson in fall. Long clusters of white flowers in late spring and early summer turn pinkish purple as they age and are beautiful among fall foliage. Stems and flower buds may be damaged if temperature falls much below –10°F/–23°C. Attractive container plant. Prune after flowering to control size.

HYPERICUM ANDROSAEMUM

10°F/–12°C. ☼ ☼ ◐ ◐ SUN, PARTIAL SHADE IN HOT AREAS, MODERATE TO REGULAR WATER. SEMIEVERGREEN SHRUB OR TALL GROUND COVER.

Clusters of golden yellow summer flowers are followed by berries that turn from red to purple to black as they age. To 3 ft. tall, with stems arching toward the top.

ITEA VIRGINICA. Virginia sweetspire

0°F/–18°C. ☼ ☼ ◐ SUN OR PARTIAL SHADE, REGULAR WATER. DECIDUOUS SHRUB.

Erect shrub to 3–5 ft. or taller, with dark green leaves that turn purplish red or bright red in fall and persist on plant for a long time, sometimes all winter in mild climates. 'Henry's Garnet' has garnet red fall color; 'Saturnalia' fall foliage is mix of orange, purple, and wine red. Fragrant clusters of creamy white flowers in spring or summer.

MISCANTHUS SINENSIS. Eulalia grass, Japanese silver grass, Maiden grass

–20°F/–29°C. ☼ ◐ SUN, MODERATE WATER. ORNAMENTAL GRASS.

Attractive flower clusters open as tassels and gradually expand into large plumes atop stalks 2–7 ft. tall in late summer or fall. Plumes are silvery to pinkish or bronze and last well into winter. Foliage is graceful; turns to shades of yellow, orange, or reddish brown in fall and winter. Cut back old foliage to ground before new growth sprouts in spring.

SEDUM SPECTABILE, S. TELEPHIUM

–20°F/–29°C. ☼ ◐ ◐ SUN, MODERATE TO REGULAR WATER. PERENNIALS.

Dense, dome-shaped clusters of pink flowers appear in late summer and fall and mature into long-lasting brownish maroon seed clusters atop 1½- to 2-ft.-tall bare stems. Many varieties, some with deep rose red or maroon flowers. Popular *S. telephium* 'Autumn Joy' has bright salmon pink blossoms that turn to russet. All die to ground in winter.

BRIGHT PLANTS FOR SHADE

Plants that have lime green or greenish gold foliage or white, yellow, or cream variegation seem to glow in the shade. The effect is useful for the otherwise gloomy areas of the garden heavily shaded by trees, fences, and buildings. White or blue flowers also brighten up a shady area.

AJUGA REPTANS. Carpet bugle
–30°F/–34°C. ☼ ◐ ● SUN OR PARTIAL SHADE, REGULAR WATER. PERENNIAL.

Spreads quickly by runners, making a mat of handsome leaves. Choose the varieties with pale leaf colorings, such as 'Multicolor' ('Rainbow'), with green leaves marbled with cream and pink; 'Variegata', green leaves with creamy yellow blotches and leaf edges; or 'Burgundy Lace' ('Burgundy Glow'), reddish purple leaves variegated with white and pink. All send up blue flower spikes in spring and early summer.

COLEUS HYBRIDUS. Coleus
◐ ☼ ● MOST TAKE SHADE, SOME FULL SUN, ALL AMPLE WATER. PERENNIAL TREATED AS ANNUAL.

Tropical plant, 1–2 ft. tall, grown for its brilliantly colored leaves. Choose plants with stripes or blotches of pale green, pink, cream, chartreuse, or yellow. Remove flower buds to ensure vigorous growth. Take cuttings (they will root in water) in early fall to continue plants into next year. Good container plant.

DAPHNE ODORA 'MARGINATA'. Winter daphne
10°F/–12°C. ◐ ☼ ● PARTIAL SHADE, SUN IN COOL-SUMMER AREAS, MODERATE WATER. EVERGREEN SHRUB.

Neat, handsome plant to 4 ft. tall and wider with nosegay clusters of intensely fragrant pink flowers at branch ends in winter. Green leaves are edged with band of yellow. A little fussy: needs well-aerated, neutral pH soil and top of rootball to sit higher than soil level.

HAKONECHLOA MACRA 'AUREOLA'. Japanese forest grass
–10°F/–23°C. ◐ ● ● PARTIAL OR FULL SHADE, REGULAR WATER. ORNAMENTAL GRASS.

Graceful, slim, arching stems to 1½ ft. carrying long, slender leaves striped with gold. Effect is that of a tiny bamboo. Spreads slowly by underground runners. Goes dormant in winter. Good container plant.

HOSTA. Plantain lily
–35°F/–37°C. ◐ ● ● PARTIAL OR FULL SHADE, REGULAR WATER. PERENNIAL.

Elegant foliage plant with heart-shaped, lance-shaped, oval, or nearly round leaves and huge range of leaf colors, including light green, chartreuse, and blue, with white, cream, or yellow variegations. Leaf texture

TOP: *Coleus hybridus*
BOTTOM: *Hostas*

also interesting: may be smooth, quilted, puckery, dull, or glossy. Dwarf plants available as short as 6 in.; giants to 5 ft. Spikes of lavender or white flowers in summer. Goes dormant in winter. Needs some winter chill. Good container plant.

LAMIUM MACULATUM. Dead nettle, spotted nettle
–20°F/–29°C. ◐ ● ● PARTIAL OR FULL SHADE, REGULAR WATER. PERENNIAL.

Vigorous ground cover to 6 in. tall with heart-shaped leaves that are grayish green with silvery markings. Pink flowers from spring into summer. Many choice varieties, including 'Beacon Silver', with green-edged, silvery gray leaves; 'White Nancy', a 'Beacon Silver' with white blooms; and 'Chequers', with white center stripe on green leaves.

PITTOSPORUM TOBIRA 'VARIEGATA'. Variegated tobira
30°F/–1°C. ☼ ☼ ● ● SUN OR PARTIAL SHADE, MODERATE TO REGULAR WATER. EVERGREEN SHRUB.

Dense, rounded shrub reaching 5–10 ft. tall unless restricted by pruning, with whorls of grayish green leaves edged with white. Creamy white flowers in early spring smell like orange blossoms. 'Turner's Dwarf' is similar but not so tall.

PULMONARIA. Lungwort
–35°F/–37°C. ◐ ● ● PARTIAL OR FULL SHADE, REGULAR WATER. PERENNIAL.

Several species and hybrids available; choose plants with silver-dappled and spotted leaves, such as *P. saccharata* 'Sissinghurst White', with white flowers; *P. s.* 'Janet Fisk', which has leaves that are silvery almost all over and blooms that turn from pink to blue; and hybrid 'Spilled Milk', which has almost solid silvery white leaves with just a few flecks of dark green. Goes dormant in winter. Flowers generally emerge in spring, just before or at same time as leaves.

VINCA MINOR. Dwarf periwinkle
–30°F/–34°C. ◐ ● ● PARTIAL OR FULL SHADE, MODERATE WATER. EVERGREEN GROUND COVER.

Spreading mat of shiny, dark green leaves, with blue, pinwheel-shaped flowers in spring. Many varieties available; choose ones with variegated foliage, such as 'Aureola', with yellow veins in leaf centers.

VERTICAL FLOWERING PLANTS

Tall, airy masses or spires of flowers can add height to your garden from spring into fall and come back year after year without the plants gaining girth or shading out the plants around them. It's fun to see plants grow quickly to a colossal size in one season and then seem to disappear until the next.

ALLIUM GIGANTEUM. Giant allium
0°F/–18°C. ☼ ◐ SUN, REGULAR WATER. DECIDUOUS BULB.

Spectacular, softball-size clusters of bright lilac blossoms on 5- to 6-ft.-tall leafless stems in summer. The plant is a relative of the edible onion, but doesn't smell of onions. Dies to ground after bloom; reemerges in following year.

ANEMONE HYBRIDA.
Japanese anemone
–20°F/–29°C. ☼ ◑ ◐ SUN OR PARTIAL SHADE, REGULAR WATER. PERENNIAL.

Graceful branching stems to 4 ft. tall or more with loose sprays of white or pink flowers in late summer and fall. Choose tallest varieties, such as 'Honorine Jobert', which has single white blossoms. Spreads readily once established.

ANGELICA ARCHANGELICA. Angelica
–30°F/–34°C. ◑ ◐ PARTIAL SHADE, REGULAR WATER. BIENNIAL.

Highly decorative herb. Produces clump of foliage in first year; in second year, sends up thick, 6-ft.-tall stems crowned with greenish white flowers in large umbrella-like clusters. Dies after blooming. For more plants, leave flowers in place to self-sow.

CANNA
20°F/–7°C. ☼ ◐ ◑◑ SUN, AMPLE WATER DURING GROWTH AND BLOOM. TUBEROUS-ROOTED PERENNIAL.

Lush tropical plant to 6 ft. tall. Large leaves like banana leaves may be green, bronze, or variegated. Wide range of flower colors, some vividly streaked and spotted. Plant blooms in summer and fall. Can be grown in a pot partially submerged in water garden. Best suited to warm-summer climates.

CIMICIFUGA RACEMOSA. Black snakeroot
–35°F/–37°C. ☼ ◑ ◐ SUN, PARTIAL SHADE, REGULAR WATER. PERENNIAL.

Refined border or woodland plant. Wands of white flowers to 7 ft. tall on slim stalks in mid- to late summer. Ornamental seed clusters follow flowers. Shiny, dark green leaves are finely divided, delicate. Will take sun if given plentiful water. Needs some winter chill.

TOP: *Angelica archangelica*
BOTTOM: *Cimicifuga racemosa*

DIERAMA PULCHERRIMUM. Fairy wand
20°F/–7°C. ☼ ◐ SUN, REGULAR WATER. CORM.

Graceful accent plant native to South Africa. Slender, arching stems to 7 ft. tall, topped with pendulous, purplish pink to pink and white bell flowers in spring or summer. Stems move in wind. Leaves evergreen, swordlike, to 2 ft. long. Form is most effective against background of dark green shrubs or on a slope, viewed from below.

FOENICULUM VULGARE 'PURPUREA', 'SMOKEY'. Bronze fennel
–20°F/–29°C. ☼ ◐ SUN, MODERATE WATER. PERENNIAL.

Feathery foliage to 6 ft. tall with coppery tints early in season, maturing to bronzy purple green. Flat clusters of yellow flowers in mid- to late summer. May self-sow aggressively, so consider removing seed heads before seeds drop. Cut back when foliage turns brown; new stems will grow in spring.

PAPAVER SOMNIFERUM. Opium poppy
☼ ◐ ◑ SUN, MODERATE TO REGULAR WATER. ANNUAL.

To 4 ft. tall, with grayish green leaves and 4- to 5-in. flowers in white or rosy shades (pink and red to purple) in late spring. Large, decorative seed capsules. Opium is derived from the sap of the green capsules; ripe ones yield the poppy seed used in baking.

VERBASCUM BOMBYCIFERUM 'ARCTIC SUMMER'. Mullein
–20°F/–29°C. ☼ ◐ SUN, MODERATE WATER. BIENNIAL.

Foot-high rosettes of broad, conspicuously furry, grayish green leaves. In summer of second year, sends up powdery white stems to 6 ft. or more, densely set with yellow flowers. Summer blooming. Leave stems in place for reseeding. A perennial mullein, *V. olympicum*, also has tall flowering stems.

VERBENA BONARIENSIS
10°F/–12°C. ☼ ◐ SUN, MODERATE WATER. PERENNIAL, OR ANNUAL IN COLD CLIMATES.

Airy, see-through plant. Produces tight clusters of little purple flowers in sprays atop 4- to 6-ft.-tall, nearly leafless stems in summer. Self-sows.

Birds and Butterflies

Birds visit a garden for seeds, berries, or nectar. Butterflies are searching for nectar, a place to lay eggs, and food for the caterpillar larvae. Most of the plants here attract both birds and butterflies. For more plant ideas, turn to the butterfly and hummingbird gardens on pages 40 and 42 and the berry-producing plants listed on page 108.

ASCLEPIAS TUBEROSA. Butterfly weed

−20°F/−29°C. ☼ ◑ SUN, MODERATE WATER. PERENNIAL. HUMMINGBIRDS, BUTTERFLY LARVAE AND ADULTS.

Stems grow to 3 ft. tall. Broad clusters of bright orange flowers form on their tops in midsummer. Flowers of Gay Butterflies strain are yellow to red. 'Hello Yellow' is a selected form and has bright yellow flowers. Foliage dies to ground in fall; new growth emerges in spring. Prefers good drainage.

BUDDLEIA DAVIDII. Butterfly bush, Summer lilac

0°F/−18°C. ☼ ◑ ● ◑ SUN OR LIGHT SHADE, MODERATE TO REGULAR WATER. DECIDUOUS OR SEMIEVERGREEN SHRUB. HUMMINGBIRDS, ADULT BUTTERFLIES.

Fast, rank growth in spring and summer to 3, 4, or even 10 ft. tall. Long, dark green, lance-shaped leaves are white and felted beneath. In midsummer, dense, arching plumes of small, fragrant flowers (lilac with orange eye) appear at branch tips, some 1 ft. long or more. Many varieties available with pink, blue, purple, or white flowers. Cut back plants severely in late winter to promote flowering and to keep the plant orderly and attractive. Can be grown as a standard.

COTONEASTER

HARDINESS VARIES. ☼ ◑ SUN, MODERATE WATER. EVERGREEN, SEMIEVERGREEN, DECIDUOUS SHRUBS AND GROUND COVERS. BIRDS.

Bears small white or pinkish springtime flowers resembling tiny single roses; not showy but pretty because abundant. Striking color is in red and orangish red berries that ripen in fall and may last through winter. Many species easy to grow, requiring little maintenance. Allow room to spread; clipping may ruin plant form. For especially showy fruit, choose deciduous *C. adpressus praecox* (creeping cotoneaster), 1½ ft. tall and 6 ft. wide, or *C. apiculatus* (cranberry cotoneaster), 3 ft. tall and 6 ft. across, both hardy to −10°F/−23°C. Two evergreens with showy fruit are *C. lacteus* (Parney cotoneaster), 10°F/−12°C, an 8-ft.-tall fountain of graceful arching branches that can be espaliered; and *C. microphyllus* (rockspray cotoneaster), 0°F/−18°C, which grows 2–3 ft. tall and 6 ft. across, with tiny leaves.

LAVANDULA. Lavender

HARDINESS VARIES. ☼ ◑ SUN, MODERATE WATER. EVERGREEN SHRUB. HUMMINGBIRDS, ADULT BUTTERFLIES.

Slender stems of fragrant lavender or purple flowers produced on domes of aromatic grayish or gray green foliage. Many species available, including the classic lavender used for perfume, *L. angustifolia* (English lavender), hardy to −10°F/−23°C, which grows to 4 ft. tall

and wide and flowers in late spring or summer; and *L. dentata* (French lavender), 20°F/−7°C, to 3 ft. tall, with short, tufted, lavender purple flower spikes over a long spring-summer blooming period. All useful as low hedge or edging.

MAHONIA

HARDINESS VARIES. ☼ ◑ ● ◑ ◑ EXPOSURE AND WATER NEEDS VARY. EVERGREEN SHRUBS. BIRDS.

Prickly-leafed, tough plants that look good all year. Bright yellow flowers in dense clusters or spikes in late winter or early spring, followed by berries, typically blue black covered with a chalky film. *M. aquifolium* (Oregon grape), hardy to 0°F/−18°C, grows to 6 ft. tall and turns bronzy, purplish, or wine red in winter; its edible fruit makes good jelly. It can take sun or shade and needs little water. *M. bealei* (leatherleaf mahonia) and *M. lomariifolia* are tall species, to 10 ft., and have striking sculptural forms. Both plants prefer partial shade and regular water.

PENSTEMON. Beard tongue

HARDINESS VARIES. ☼ ◑ ◑ ◑ SUN, AFTERNOON SHADE IN HOT CLIMATES, MODERATE TO REGULAR WATER. PERENNIAL. HUMMINGBIRDS.

Produces long, loose spikes of flaring, tubular flowers, most commonly bright red or blue but can be white, yellow, lilac, purple, or many shades of pink. *P. barbatus*, hardy to −20°F/−29°C, has an open, sprawling habit to 3 ft. tall and flowers in midsummer to early fall. *P. digitalis*, −40°F/−40°C, grows to 5 ft. tall and flowers in spring to early summer; one variety, 'Husker Red', 2½–3 ft. tall, has maroon leaves, pale pink flowers. *P. gloxinioides* (border or garden penstemon), 9°F/−13°C, is compact, bushy, upright to 2–4 ft., and blooms in summer in almost all colors but blue and yellow. Most penstemons not suited to Gulf Coast and Florida.

SALVIA. Sage, salvia

HARDINESS VARIES. ☼ ◑ MOST PREFER SUN AND REGULAR WATER. LISTED PLANTS ARE PERENNIALS. HUMMINGBIRDS, ADULT BUTTERFLIES.

Diverse range of plants, many with spikes of red or blue tubular flowers and coarse, aromatic leaves. *S. azurea grandiflora*, hardy to 10°F/−12°C, grows to 5 ft. tall and provides a mass of blue flowers from summer to first frost. *S. coccinea*, to 2–3 ft. tall, usually grown as self-seeding annual, has dark green, furry leaves and red flowers from spring into fall. *S. splendens* (scarlet sage), 1–3 ft. tall, also usually grown as an annual, has bright green foliage and scarlet flowers in tall, dense clusters in summer.

INDEX

Page numbers in **boldface** refer to photographs.